The Peace That Never Was

The Peace That Never Was

A History of the League of Nations

Ruth Henig

Published in 2019 by
Haus Publishing Ltd
4 Cinnamon Row
London SW11 3TW
www.hauspublishing.com

A previous edition was published in 2010

A CIP catalogue record for this book
is available from the British Library

ISBN 978-1-910376-78-2
eISBN 978-1-912208-56-2

Typeset in Sabon by MacGuru Ltd
Printed in Great Britain by TJ International Ltd
Maps by Martin Lubikowski, ML Design, London

Contents

For Samuel, Lucy, Bobby and Eric

Acknowledgements

My greatest debt is to Professor Alan Sharp, who has suggested for many years that I should write a history of the League of Nations, and who finally found a way of bringing it about. I would like to thank him and Jen for their friendship, hospitality and intellectual stimulation over more years than I care to remember. I would also like to thank Mark Rowe for sending me books and articles relating to the League and for his interest in the progress of the manuscript. Barbara Schwepcke of Haus Publishing has been consistently helpful and supportive, and I would also like to thank Jaqueline Mitchell for dealing so calmly with my rather erratic early drafts and for all her help with the pictures and the text. Finally, this book would not have been completed without the unfailing support and encouragement of my husband, Jack, who was always ready to cheer me up or to carry me off to a nearby hostelry when I needed a break from writing. Needless to say, neither he nor the alcohol are to blame for any remaining errors of fact or of punctuation in the final text.

Preface

When I started writing about the League of Nations 50 years ago, there was general agreement amongst diplomatic historians that the League was a total failure. Its central task had been to prevent the outbreak of another major war, and it had comprehensively failed. A J P Taylor, a historian of very decided views, declared that in the study of the inter-war period, the League was a complete 'irrelevance'. More recently, in her major book *Peacemakers*, published in 2001, Canadian historian Margaret MacMillan commented witheringly that 'only a handful of eccentric historians still bother to study the League of Nations'.

The focus of enquiry in the 1960s and 1970s was therefore on the causes of League failure. Broadly speaking, two main lines of analysis were pursued. On the one hand, it was argued that states had failed to live up to the commitments they had agreed to in the League Covenant – they paid lip service to them, but in practice were driven by national ambition, greed and self-interest. Many who took this view were European left-wing idealists, or American admirers of Woodrow Wilson who believed that the American President's attempts to construct a better world after 1919 were sabotaged by European leaders. A second group argued that, on the contrary, the aims of the League were far too ambitious and idealistic, and were inevitably undermined by considerations of realpolitik. Viewed from this perspective, Wilson was not the hero but the villain, and his scheme of guaranteeing League members' territorial integrity and political independence, plus the pursuit of unrealistic schemes of armament limitation, were seen as unachievable in a world of competing great powers. Some argued that a more limited scheme of international co-operation might have worked, but basically, as Wittgenstein commented, to assess why the League failed, historians first needed to find out 'why wolves eat lambs'. So the best that could be said of the League in the decades immediately after the Second World War was that it had at least laid the foundations for the United Nations and its range of ancillary bodies, and that the United Nations would hopefully succeed where the League had failed in bringing lasting peace and prosperity to an exhausted world.

Fast-forward 50 years, and the League is being viewed by a range of younger historians in a very different and more positive light. In the first instance, the United Nations has faced similar problems to the League in relation to conflict resolution and arms limitation. Its peacekeeping record makes the League's settlement of a range of territorial disputes in the 1920s appear very respectable. Secondly, we can now see much more clearly than was possible in the 1950s and 60s that the Great War of 1914–18 unleashed such powerful tremors across the globe, a veritable tsunami, that many historians now claim that it was not until the early 1990s that the full effects of the conflict finally subsided. Thus the impact of the Great War did not just destabilise the inter-war period, but caused serious international instability for at least 30 years thereafter. How could the League possibly operate effectively in such a volatile and hostile environment? But just because it had inevitably failed to prevent renewed conflict after 1919 was not a reason for ignoring its successes in other aspects of its work. Rather than judging the League on one area of its activities, however important, historians now argue that a wider view should be taken of the League's activities, acknowledging that in many diverse fields it was extremely successful. Thus, in the past two decades, the League has been portrayed in an increasingly positive light. Given the circumstances of its birth, given that it was a very complex organisation offering not just a variety of routes of escape from war but an unprecedented level of inter-state co-operation across a wide variety of fields, and given its early abandonment by the United States, much of its work is now seen as pioneering and as of considerable importance. Crucially, it helped to establish internationally accepted norms of conduct between sovereign states in relation to minority rights, trusteeship principles and the establishment and safeguarding of human rights. The horrors of the Second World War only served to underline just how important it was for states to agree to uphold such norms both in their internal and external activities; thus the development of recent human rights legislation, concepts of minority rights and of orderly transition to statehood can be traced back in origin to the work of the League.

Furthermore, the League's work in the fields of humanitarian relief, exchange of populations, international labour organisation, the establishment of an international court, financial and economic co-operation, the combatting of global health epidemics and the drugs trade and a whole host of other humanitarian activities were all truly groundbreaking, and continue to this day through United Nations agencies and other global bodies. Even more innovative was the establishment of the League Secretariat and the rise of the international civil servant and the NGO expert – here, the League paved the way for our modern international landscape and for a range of international bodies and initiatives, including the European Union. As Lord Cecil pointed out at the League's last meeting in 1946, 'The work of the League is purely and unmistakeably printed on the social, economic and humanitarian life of the world.' That is even more true today than it was in 1946. The League was indeed the world's first major international global organisation.

A new generation of historians is arguing that the League's importance lies in the fact that it set in motion a different dynamic of international co-operation. Despite the enduring problem that competing national interests are by no means easy to reconcile, the League succeeded in laying the groundwork, in Susan Pederson's words, for 'that fragile network of norms and agreements by which our world is now regulated if not quite governed'. Looked at in a different way, the League system can be seen, in the words of Clive Archer, as a crucial link 'bringing together the strands of pre-1914 international organisation and wartime co-operation into a more centralised and systematic form on a global scale, thus providing a stepping stone towards the more enduring United Nations'. Recent scholarship has emphasised the importance of the League in influencing the behaviour of states and the shape of the international system, through the effect of the 'Geneva atmosphere' on those who negotiated there and, equally as crucially, on those who aspired to join the 'Geneva club'.

So having – rather eccentrically in the eyes of some academic colleagues – embarked on the study of a widely discredited body in the late 1960s, I now regard myself as a far-sighted pioneer, both in choosing to study the workings of the League, and in my enduring belief that the League has a lot to teach the contemporary world about the possibilities and pitfalls of establishing a more regulated and co-operative international community in an increasingly fragmented land-scape of national entities. This concise history of the League aims to present a balanced account of the 20th century's first international organisation with global reach, by analysing its failures and at the same time documenting its significant achievements. It is my contribution to the overdue rehabilita-tion of this great 'international experiment' and of its endur-ing legacy.

1
One Vision – Many Approaches

For centuries, philosophers and statesmen had dreamed of constructing inter-state systems or international frameworks to promote harmony and preserve peace amongst potentially antagonistic states. But it took the four long years of appalling waste and senseless slaughter on the battlefields of the First World War before such dreams were translated into reality, and the construction of a League of Nations was catapulted to the top of the peace agenda in January 1919.

Looking back to the immediate aftermath of the war, it is clear that the international environment of 1919–20 could not have been less auspicious for the birth of the world's first truly international organisation. The impact of the First World War was far-reaching and long-lasting; much of the damage was immediately visible, such as the sudden end of four great empires, massive financial indebtedness amongst nations, the outbreak of revolutions and of serious social unrest not just in Europe but across the globe, and not least the obvious physical damage in the shape of the scarred battlegrounds and devastated regions of France and Belgium.

But many historians also argue that the prolonged conflict

had profound social, economic and political effects which persisted for decades, and that it was only in the 1990s that Western societies began fully to recover from the shock of the First World War.[1] However, precisely because of the enormous damage that the war had caused, it was imperative that a League of Nations was constructed as quickly as possible. Its establishment would be one of the few tangible gains of the war, serving as a symbol of hope for millions of bereaved families, displaced individuals and fleeing refugees that their sacrifices had not been in vain, and that the end of the First World War would truly bring about lasting peace amongst nations.

Whilst the war was undoubtedly the most important catalyst in the establishment of the League of Nations, there were a number of significant developments in the late 19th and early 20th centuries which highlighted the need for an international body which could broker agreements between states on specific issues or on problems which were proving particularly difficult to solve. The scientific and technological revolution which gathered pace in the second half of the 19th century created the need for a network of international agreements, all of which required central co-ordination, to oversee worldwide postal deliveries, lay cables and link telegraph systems and regulate major waterways, amongst other things. Over 300 international conferences were held to discuss such issues as sanitation, police regulations, patents, copyrights, the standardisation of weights and measures, agricultural and commercial issues, and the establishment and operation of the International Red Cross.[2] The spread of free trade around the globe and the opening up of markets led to an increase in the numbers of commercial treaties between states, and to the provision of informal mechanisms through which disputes could be arbitrated.

The use of arbitration to resolve disputes, not just of a non-political nature but increasingly intractable political issues, grew markedly at the end of the 19th century and in the first decade of the 20th. The United States and Britain were able to resolve a number of differences fairly amicably after the American Civil War, most notably the claims arising out of the damage inflicted during that conflict by the Confederate warship *Alabama*, built in the shipyards of Birkenhead, which the British Prime Minister Herbert Gladstone agreed to settle through arbitration in 1871. Between 1899 and 1903, some 20 governments signed arbitral agreements; and by 1914, 100 arbitration treaties were in force.[3] The use of arbitration treaties as a valuable means of resolving potential disputes between states was very strongly advocated in the United States, and the US Secretary of State from 1905–8, Elihu Root, who had enjoyed a distinguished legal career, was responsible for concluding some 40 reciprocal arbitration treaties which eventually covered 24 countries. However, it had become very clear before 1914 that the process of arbitration had its limitations. It could deal effectively with disputes arising from legal issues or misunderstandings relating to treaty provisions, but Root's agreements could not extend to matters involving national honour, vital interest or independence. The American Senate took a close interest in negotiations, and insisted on the right to approve, in each case, the agreement on which particular issues were to be the subject of arbitration. And while informed opinion in the United States continued to favour the use of arbitration to resolve international disputes, the United States Government, in the early years of the 20th century, refused to submit three outstanding controversies to arbitral settlement, two relating to Panama and one to an ongoing dispute with Mexico.[4]

The limits of arbitration as a means of resolving disputes between nations were highlighted very graphically under the US Presidency of William Howard Taft, who took office in 1908. Like Root, he had enjoyed a distinguished judicial career, and in his new position he was keen to further the idea of world peace through the process of arbitration. His ultimate goal was to help to establish 'an arbitral court whose jurisdiction should be increased ultimately to include all possible disputes of an international character' and he proceeded to negotiate treaties with Canada, Britain and France in which the parties would arbitrate all justiciable disputes. While the negotiations with Canada eventually failed, a more serious obstacle was the insistence of the American Senate that disputes arising from issues such as immigration, state indebtedness and the Monroe Doctrine could not be included.

Leading Republicans such as the former President Theodore Roosevelt and Senator Henry Cabot Lodge expressed their strong view that there were circumstances in which the United States would choose to fight over differences with other states, rather than resort to arbitration or negotiation. In the end, the Senate approved a reservation excluding certain types of disputes from consideration by the projected arbitration treaties, before approving their conclusion. In a telling comment, anticipating the later problems which arose in the United States over ratification of the League Covenant, a United States internationalist observed in 1912 that 'we cannot enter into international agreements and at the same time maintain intact in every respect what is called sovereign power or senatorial prerogative'.[5]

The first Hague Conference, held in 1899, boosted calls for an international arbitral tribunal or world Supreme Court. Convened by Tsar Nicholas II of Russia primarily to discuss means of limiting, and if possible reducing, the growth of armaments between nations, the 26 states which attended, (which included mainly European states, but also the United States, Mexico and five Asian countries) were also tasked to examine how best to advance the pacific settlement of disputes. There was general agreement on what the rules of arbitration should be, and that a Permanent Court of Arbitration should be set up, but in practice this only amounted to the establishment of a panel of judges who would be willing to resolve disputes through arbitration if any were to be submitted to them. The 'Court' would have no power to enforce decrees, though it was given administrative machinery to provide a permanent framework for any tribunals which might be required, and each state would retain full sovereignty to decide whether they wished to avail themselves of the service or not.

The final convention adopted by the Hague Conference also included a provision for the appointment of 'International Commissions of Enquiry' which might help to resolve disputes arising not from matters of national honour or of vital interest but involving differences of opinion on points of fact. Five years later, this diplomatic mechanism proved invaluable in resolving the 'Dogger Bank' incident during which the Russian fleet, on its way to fight Japan in the Far East, fired on some British fishing vessels, having mistaken them for enemy ships.[6]

Thus it appeared that a promising start had been made. Four cases were brought before the Hague Arbitration Court in the first few years of the 20th century, and many internationalists hoped that further such gatherings at the Hague might crystallise into 'a permanent and recognised advisory Congress of Nations'. One Congressman, Richard Bartholdt, even suggested the members of such a body should agree to respect each other's 'territorial and political integrity', and that armed forces of the nations represented should be at the service of the Congress to enforce any decree which the Hague Court might issue in accordance with treaties of arbitration.[7]

The annual meeting of the Inter-Parliamentary Union, a body established in 1889 to enable members of parliaments and assemblies from different countries to meet regularly, recommended in 1905 that a further Hague Conference should be held, and raised the possibility of a reorganised Inter-Parliamentary Union becoming a representative arm of a Hague Conference which would meet on a regular basis. In 1907, a second Hague Conference was convened, a much bigger gathering than the first, with 256 delegates from 44 countries. But the greater number of countries represented made it more, not less, difficult to reach agreement on issues such as general treaties of arbitration or the establishment of a more permanent Court of International Justice, since all decisions had to be unanimous. Some discussions on the rules of warfare and on questions of neutral rights did result in general agreement, but disagreements on how to select the judges prevented any progress on the establishment of a Permanent Court of International Justice. While there were hopes that a further Hague Conference might be called, the international climate in the years leading up to 1914 made this increasingly unlikely.

Nonetheless, influential figures in the United States remained convinced that arbitration offered the most promising means of resolving international disputes and promoting world peace. Ex-President Theodore Roosevelt emphasised to the Nobel Committee, in 1910, the importance of arbitration treaties and of strengthening the Hague Court. He believed the Great Powers 'should form a League of Peace to keep peace amongst themselves and prevent it being broken by others'.[8]

The wealthy American industrialist, Andrew Carnegie, returning to his native Scotland in 1905 to address the students of St Andrews who had elected him as Rector, called for a League of Peace to try to stop wars. Two years later he used the phrase 'League of Nations' to describe an international entity which could call on an international force similar to that which quelled the Boxer Uprising in China in 1900.[9] In 1910, Carnegie used some of his considerable wealth to set up the Carnegie Endowment for International Peace with a $10 million endowment and Elihu Root as its first president. He and many other United States internationalists tried to advance the use of arbitration by the Hague mechanism, and to reinforce President Taft's efforts to persuade the United States government to submit disputes to arbitral processes. William Jennings Bryan, President Woodrow Wilson's first Secretary of State, followed a somewhat different course after 1913, promoting a series of bilateral treaties aimed to resolve any disputes that might arise between the signatories by resort to a standing International Commission of Enquiry, and by using 'cooling off periods'. The treaty signatories pledged themselves not to go to war for a period of 12 months, during which time investigations could take place and attempts be made to deal with the problem through arbitration. Bryan claimed to have used this approach successfully many years previously to resolve labour disputes, and was convinced that a 'cooling-off period' of twelve months would allow tempers to calm and would facilitate peaceful negotiations. Within a year, over 20 treaties had been negotiated, with countries which included Britain and France. Significantly, however, the German government refused to follow suit.[10]

In the years before 1914, especially on the European mainland, there was markedly less confidence in the possible efficacy of arbitration, or of 'cooling off' processes, and growing pessimism about the ability of any international mechanisms to resolve inter-state disputes. In 19th-century Europe, the leading powers attempted to resolve conflicts, particularly amongst smaller powers, by working collaboratively through the Congress system or 'Concert of Europe', established after the Vienna settlement of 1815 at the end of the Napoleonic wars. Meeting periodically to deal with problems of mutual concern, the major powers in Europe came together on a number of occasions during the 19th century to deal with sudden diplomatic crises or to settle thorny and contested issues. The 'Concert of Europe' successfully adjudicated on claims arising from the European 'scramble for Africa' in the 1870s and early 1880s, and spent much time and energy trying to resolve or to limit a number of contentious territorial disputes in eastern and south-eastern Europe arising from the inexorable decline of the Ottoman Empire. However, the system could only work if individual states took the lead in convening a meeting to resolve or to head off a crisis, and the other major powers were prepared to respond. There was no machinery to compel states to attend or to ensure that meetings were held at regular intervals.

As Europe became dangerously divided between two Great Power 'blocs' in the early years of the 20th century, and as levels of military preparedness and of armaments rose alarmingly, willingness to submit disputes and grievances to a conference of powers declined. The outbreak of two Balkan Wars, fuelling Serbian nationalism and posing a serious threat to the stability of the Austro-Hungarian Empire, was followed by a conference at which the major European powers exerted pressure over the belligerent Balkan states to prevent them from engaging in further hostilities, and to stop themselves from being dragged into the series of conflicts. But the assassination of the Austrian Crown Prince Franz Ferdinand in Sarajevo in June 1914 triggered a sequence of events which proved far more difficult to contain.

As war clouds gathered, the British government, through its Foreign Secretary Edward Grey, desperately tried to convene a conference of the leading European powers to try to resolve the crisis, but could not persuade the German or Austro-Hungarian governments to attend. In early August, 1914, a large number of European powers found themselves instead drawn into a war which lasted for much longer and cost far more in both human and material resources than anyone had imagined to be possible in 1914. And as the war escalated, Grey and the British government became ever more convinced that the First World War would not have broken out had there been an international body in existence in 1914 which could have compelled states to submit their disputes for discussion and potential resolution according to a set of agreed procedures.

A number of influential individuals close to the Liberal Government shared this view. Viscount Bryce, who had been a Liberal MP for 27 years before serving as Ambassador to the United States between 1907 and 1913, and a group of like-minded international pacifists, who included the Cambridge historian and writer Goldsworthy Lowes Dickinson and the Liberal MP Sir Willoughby Dickinson, met regularly after the outbreak of the war to discuss and try to formulate a set of principles on which an international body to preserve peace between nations might be based. As the war intensified and resulted in increasing numbers of casualties, the group, in February 1915, produced a set of 'Proposals for the Avoidance of War'. They advocated that an international court of justice or the Hague Court of Arbitration should deal with justiciable disputes. A 'Council of Conciliation' should consider all other disputes. While this took place, the affected states should agree not to resort to war within a year, or within six months after an award or report from the international body. All the other signatory powers should take sanctions of an economic or more 'forcible' kind against a state failing to abide by these agreements. The Council could take action if peace was threatened in any way, even if the parties most directly involved did not refer their quarrels to it, and it could also propose programmes of disarmament.[11]

As the British Ambassador to the United States, Bryce had forged close links with Presidents Roosevelt and Taft, and with Secretaries of State Root and Bryan. The ideas of his group were quickly circulated around the 60 or more peace groups which existed in the United States at the outbreak of the war. Some of these, such as the American Peace Society and the Carnegie Endowment for International Peace, believed that the most promising route to secure international peace lay through the adoption of judicial processes such as arbitral courts and a determined push towards the codification of international law which states would agree to observe. Other groups, however, felt that concerted political pressure was also required to maintain peace amongst sovereign states. In 1915, around 300 leading peace campaigners, meeting at Philadelphia, agreed to a series of proposals which were very much influenced both by the Bryan treaties and by the proposals of the Bryce group.

A League was to be established of all the great nations and some medium-sized powers, to ensure that they submitted justiciable disputes to a judicial tribunal and non-justiciable disputes to a Council of Conciliation, for 'hearing, consideration and recommendation'. Force, either economic or military, would be used by League members to compel states to submit any disputes to the appropriate body. But the League would also encourage the rule of law to spread by holding conferences from time to time to formulate and to codify the rules of international law. A new organisation, the 'League to Enforce Peace', was set up to campaign nationwide and further afield on the basis of these proposals, designed, as one of its leading advocates said, to establish a League which could 'compel enquiry before nations are allowed to fight'.[12] For the next three years, League campaigners worked tirelessly to spread their ideas across the United States, and to bring their influence to bear particularly on Senators, whose role would be decisive in supporting or rejecting any United States bid to join a new international body. Would Senators, especially Republican ones, support the concept of a League which could commit the United States to war, and which might allow European powers to interfere in the affairs of Central and South America? Clearly, the role and functions of such a League, and the potential actions the United States might be asked to carry out as a member of it, were bound to arouse considerable controversy in a country whose involvement in international diplomacy had been so limited before 1914. Accordingly, supporters of the peace programme of the League to Enforce Peace worked hard to distribute their leaflets and to explain them to their fellow citizens across the United States. By early 1917, they had distributed over a million copies of League literature.[13] They were particularly keen to press their ideas on Woodrow Wilson who, before taking office as President in 1913, had been a member of the American Peace Society and a supporter of Taft's arbitration treaties. The outbreak of war in Europe in 1914 confirmed to Wilson how bankrupt European diplomacy had become, because it lacked any organised machinery for international co-operation.

Soon after, Wilson wrote to his brother-in-law that 'there must be an association of the nations, all bound together for the protection of the integrity of each, so that any one nation breaking from this bond will bring upon herself war; that is to say, punishment, automatically'.[14] In December, 1914, he and his close friend and advisor Colonel Edward M House started to draft a scheme in which the republics of North and South America would agree on a form of international co-operation to preserve peace 'which in itself would serve as a model for the European nations' when the fighting stopped. The basis of the scheme was that the states involved agreed to guarantee each others' 'political independence under republican forms of government' and territorial integrity. Negotiations were begun with three South American states with the aim of concluding a Pan-American Pact along these lines, but the scheme ran into difficulties.[15] Nonetheless, Wilson was now convinced that the agreement of states to offer guarantees of political independence and territorial integrity to fellow members could form the core of a scheme of international co-operation.

Wilson agreed to address the first annual meeting of supporters of the League to Enforce Peace in Washington in May 1916. While he spoke in generalities and avoided making any detailed commitments, he took the opportunity to commit the United States to help create a League of Nations at the end of the war, and talked of the need to respect the territorial and political integrity of nations, and to prevent future conflicts by forming an international association in which the United States would be a member. He thus became the first head of government to declare firmly in favour of a League of Nations, and this avowed support for the establishment of a new international body was an important theme in his successful re-election campaign later in the year.

Woodrow Wilson's strong advocacy of a League was enthusiastically received not just in the United States but also in Britain, where, by 1916, many groups were campaigning to gain support for schemes which they hoped would prevent the carnage of the First World War from ever happening again. The British League of Nations Society had been formed in 1915, with many of its founder members influenced by the proposals of the Bryce group, while the Union for Democratic Control was formed early in the war to press for open diplomacy and for parliamentary control of foreign policy. Its members supported Wilson's ideas, but felt that they would not be successfully implemented until diplomacy had been brought under full democratic control. Trade unionists and members of the Labour Party were also influenced by Wilson's vision, but believed that a League should represent people, not governments. The Labour Party's representative in the War Cabinet in the later stages of the war, George Barnes, agreed with Wilson's idea of a League based on guarantees of political independence and territorial integrity, but thought that it would also need an international army and supranational powers over member states if wars were to be prevented. The writer H G Wells' League was also firmly in control of armies, air forces and armament industries, while that of the economist J A Hobson was to have wide powers of intervention in economic matters and the ability to draw on the economic resources and armed forces of League members for the enforcement of its decisions.

A more limited League was proposed by Leonard Woolf in the 1916 Fabian Society publication *International Government*. He argued that while 'the rule that every dispute in which negotiation has failed must come before either a tribunal or a Conference will be the pivot of the international system', sovereign states would agree to be bound by conference or tribunal decisions only 'where the decision would not affect the independence or territorial integrity, or would not require an alteration in the internal laws of the State'. Woolf was scathing about the likelihood of any more ambitious approach being successful, writing 'It is hardly practical, in the present condition of the world, to discuss the possibility of anything like a permanent international police force ... We are only just feeling about for an International Authority, and all that we can hope for at this stage is that the nations will agree upon and declare what methods the Authority has the right to use in order to enforce those fundamental obligations upon which this system of international society rests'.[16]

By the beginning of 1917, the territorial spread of the fighting and the complexity on the Allied side of co-ordinating military action, enforcing a strong blockade against the Central Powers, and distributing amongst themselves vital but scarce resources, had both shown the possibilities of more extended international co-operation and revealed potential weapons against recalcitrant powers. In May 1915 Lord Robert Cecil, the third son of former Conservative Prime Minister the Marquis of Salisbury, joined the first coalition government of the war, as Under-Secretary of State for Foreign Affairs with particular responsibility for overseeing the Allied blockade.

He was both shocked by the devastation which the First World War was causing and struck by the possibilities of concerted international economic action. In the autumn of 1916, he presented to the Cabinet a *Memorandum on Proposals for Diminishing the Occasion of Future Wars.*

While Cecil supported the ideas of the Bryce group for an international organisation based on a clear set of rules agreed by its members, the events of June and July 1914 had shown him that 'no machinery exists to force unwilling Powers to agree to a conference and await its decision ... If, however, an instrument could be found which would exert considerable pressure on a recalcitrant Power without causing excessive risk to the Powers using it, a solution of the difficulty might perhaps be found. I believe that in blockade as developed in this war such an instrument exists. No doubt for its full effect an overwhelming naval power is requisite. But much could be done even by overwhelming financial power, and with the two combined no modern State could ultimately resist its pressure'.[17]

With the formation of the Lloyd George government in late 1916, Cecil's cousin, the former Conservative Prime Minister Arthur Balfour, was appointed Foreign Secretary. In 1917, Cecil persuaded him to set up a committee under the distinguished international lawyer Lord Phillimore to examine all the proposals for a League of Nations which had by then been advocated and to formulate a practicable scheme. The Phillimore Committee, comprising, in addition to its chairman, three prominent members of the Foreign Office and three historians, two of whom were specialists in naval history, held a number of meetings, surveyed the considerable literature which by then had been produced on the subject of post-war international organisation and proceeded to issue an interim report, followed by the final Phillimore Report, in the first half of 1918. Their conception was of an institutionalised and expanded Concert of Europe, an international body which would meet on a regular basis and whose members would agree not to resort to war without first submitting any dispute to arbitration or enquiry by a conference of fellow states and waiting for a report to be produced. The Phillimore Report did not outlaw war. Its proposals were designed to enforce a delay in a crisis, while tempers cooled and the matters in dispute could be examined dispassionately. If the members who considered the issues could not agree on a solution, or if they were able to issue a report which was duly considered and then rejected by the aggrieved power, then war could be waged after an interval of some months. The members of the Phillimore Committee did not believe that it was possible to prevent all wars, but what their proposals were designed to do was to limit conflicts and minimise their spread. Like Grey, they believed that had it been possible to force the European powers to attend a conference in the weeks before August 1914, a war involving all the European Great Powers would not have broken out. The Phillimore Report agreed with Cecil on the need for economic and then military sanctions to be brought into play, but only against an individual power which refused to abide by the agreed procedures, and resorted to war without waiting for the requisite period of time.[18]

In 1918 the French also set up an official committee to study proposals for a post-war international body, headed by a distinguished French Senator and long-time peace campaigner, Leon Bourgeois. Bourgeois was France's chief representative at both of the pre-war Hague Conferences, pushing strongly for the establishment of a permanent Court of Arbitration.

Now he turned his attention to the construction of an international body which would be equipped to stop nations from resorting to war in the future. Whereas Lord Phillimore's League relied on processes of conciliation and of delay, the French organisation proposed a range of diplomatic, legal, economic and military sanctions to compel member states to abide by its decisions. Military action could be undertaken either by forces supplied by member states, or by an international force with a permanent international staff based at the League's headquarters, whose job would be to 'deal with everything relating to the organisation of the joint forces and the eventual conduct of military operations'. It would also have the task of 'inspecting international forces and armaments in agreement with the military authorities of each State, and of proposing any improvements it may deem necessary...'.[19] Clearly, French experience since the mid 19th century led Bourgeois's commission to the view that only armed forces acting resolutely at the behest of an international body would be able to prevent the outbreak of war in the future.

While high-ranking politicians and government officials in Britain and France were researching and formulating relatively detailed schemes for a League, no similar work was undertaken by the State Department or by officials in government circles in the United States. Yet United States entry into the war on the Allied side in April 1917 had greatly raised the profile of the League enterprise, with President Wilson as its strongest advocate. His energies were focused not so much on winning the war but on the shape of the peace settlement after it which he would take the lead in drawing up. That a League would be created, and that its construction would be one of the main tasks of a peace conference, was a certainty once the United States entered the war. But what sort of body it would be was much less clear, because Wilson was reluctant to become involved in discussions of detail at this stage. He told House that he considered it extremely important for the League to 'grow and not be made; ... we must begin with solemn covenants, covering mutual guarantees of political independence and territorial integrity' and the League would then develop in authority as cases arose. The problem facing Wilson was of course clear. The American Senate 'would never ratify any treaty which put the forces of the United States at the disposal of any such group or body... Why begin at the impossible end when there is a possible end and it is feasible to plant a system which will slowly but surely ripen into fruition?' [20]

And so, rather than entrusting the State Department with the investigation and advancement of the League project, Wilson asked Colonel House to develop a feasible scheme, as part of his consideration of United States post-war conference policies. House had the benefit of reading not just the final draft of the scheme for an international body published by the League to Enforce Peace in January 1918, but also the Phillimore and Bourgeois Reports. However, he was well aware that the French scheme would raise almost impossible constitutional problems for the United States and that Wilson's view was that in a post-war world of democratic Great Powers, the moral pressure of world public opinion would be a powerful enough weapon against aggression. If it failed, the hope was that the economic sanctions which were proving so effective against the Central Powers would act as a forceful back-up. The British proposals, on the other hand, did not go far enough for Wilson.

He thought they lacked 'teeth' because they did not include the mutual exchange of territorial guarantees which, in Wilson's view, had to constitute the irreducible minimum core of any post-war international organisation. He had already made this clear in the Fourteen Points, a peace programme outlined in a speech to the United States Congress in January 1918, which famously called for the establishment of a 'general association of nations ... under specific covenants for the purposes of affording mutual guarantees of political independence and territorial integrity to great and small states alike'. Significantly, in a speech delivered in London three days earlier, the British Prime Minister David Lloyd George had outlined the task of 'some future organisation after the war' in much more general terms to be 'to limit the burden of armaments and diminish the probability of war'.[21]

In the summer of 1918, House set to work with the help of David Hunter Miller, who was the law partner of his son-in-law, and on 16 July 1918 he produced for Wilson 'Suggestions for a Covenant of a League of Nations'. His proposals were based on the relatively cautious schemes of the League to Enforce Peace and the Phillimore Committee, but inevitably he also included a provision that the Contracting Parties would 'unite in several guarantees to each other of their territorial integrity and political independence'. However, House was alert to the dangers which Cecil and others in Britain had already recognised in this approach, since he added that the guarantee scheme would be subject to 'such territorial modifications, if any, as may become necessary in the future'. House's Suggestions also included the principle that 'any war or threat of war is a matter of concern to the League' and that signatory states should disarm 'to the lowest point consistent with safety', with a disarmament plan being drawn up by a delegate conference which would only bind those states who expressly accepted it. The League should have a permanent secretariat, and a permanent international court of 15 judges who would consider cases submitted to it.[22]

With the exception of the international court, Wilson incorporated House's main proposals into his own first draft of a League Covenant. At the same time, House's diary reveals that in early August the two men decided that Wilson should insist at the peace table that a League be incorporated into the peace treaty and not left as a separate entity. Within two months, the Germans were signifying to the American President their willingness to sue for peace on the basis of his Fourteen Points, thus ensuring that the plans of Wilson and House would take centre stage in the ensuing peace negotiations. At the same time, however, in the United States Wilson was facing the run-up to the mid-term elections, and his appeal to the American people to return a Democratic majority to Congress and thus enable him to 'speak with full and undivided authority' at the forthcoming Peace Conference was attacked by political opponents as being unacceptably partisan and was decisively rejected. Whereas before the election, the Democratic Party had been in control of both Houses, after November the Republicans enjoyed a considerable majority in the House of Representatives and, most crucially, a tiny majority of two in the Senate.[23]

With his political credibility therefore badly damaged, but his political resolve stronger than ever, Wilson left the United States on 5 December to head up the peace negotiations in Europe in person, the first President ever to leave his country to undertake such an ambitious mission. The United States delegates he chose to accompany him included, apart from Colonel House, his Secretary of State Robert Lansing and General Tasker Bliss, who was the American permanent military representative at the Supreme War Council and had been

US Army Chief of Staff until May 1918. Significantly, none of them had been actively involved in the American internationalist movement and there was no place for a leading Republican representative who might have been able to feed back information to his party about the progress of the peace negotiations or exercise influence in later Senate discussions.

On arrival in Europe, Wilson received a rapturous reception from the crowds who flocked to see him in France, Italy and Britain. They cheered his declarations that open diplomacy was replacing secret diplomacy, and that the diplomacy of peoples was replacing the diplomacy of cabinets. Inevitably, the Allied leaders, David Lloyd George, Georges Clemenceau and Vittorio Orlando did not share the enthusiasm of their electorates, and were determined to try to wrest the diplomatic and political initiative from Wilson in the run-up to the opening of peace negotiations. As his main press advisor, Ray Stannard Baker, noted in his diary on 14 December, the struggle would be a fierce and difficult one for the President. 'The masses are with him to a man, but he is going to have the struggle of his life with these ugly old forces of reaction – sly, greedy, and devilishly clever.' [24] In the next chapter, we shall see how this struggle manifested itself in terms of the establishment of a League of Nations.

2

The Drafting of the Covenant, Paris, 1919

January 1919 found Woodrow Wilson in an immensely powerful position as peace negotiations began. The Germans had sued for peace on the basis of his peace programme. The impoverished Allied powers, Britain, France and Italy (together with their former ally, Tsarist Russia) collectively owed the United States nearly $8 billion, of which Britain, the wartime paymaster for its European allies – lending them more than $7 billion – owed half. In addition to financial and economic strength, the United States also deployed growing military and naval power. In September 1916, Congress voted a huge naval appropriation bill, which provided for the construction of 137 vessels of all classes. This was bound to be viewed as a provocative move by the British government. The United States' entry into the war in 1917 postponed the outbreak of a serious naval race between the two powers, but the threat to Britain's naval predominance was very clear. As Colonel House told Lloyd George bluntly at the end of the war: 'It was not our purpose to go into a naval building rivalry with Great Britain, but it was our purpose to have our rights at sea adequately safeguarded, and we did not intend to have our commerce regulated by Great Britain whenever she was at war ... sooner or later we would come to a clash if an understanding was not reached as to laws governing the seas.'[1]

Thus Wilson's strong sense of moral right and determination to conclude a just peace was reinforced by the growing power of the United States; this combination, which inevitably made him the dominating figure at the Peace Conference, posed a daunting challenge to Lloyd George, Clemenceau and Orlando, who had vital national objectives of their own to pursue. The strategy which seemed to the British government to offer the best chance of success was forcefully argued by Jan Christian Smuts, the South African statesman and former soldier now representing his Dominion on the Imperial War Cabinet, in a paper presented to the Cabinet in mid-December: 'We must from the very start of the Conference co-operate with America, and encourage and support President Wilson ... we could best signalise that co-operation by supporting President Wilson's policy of a League of Nations, and indeed by going further and giving form and substance to his rather nebulous ideas.'[2] And Smuts proceeded to do just that in an accompanying pamphlet, *The League of Nations: A Practical Suggestion*, which Lloyd George subsequently described as 'the ablest state paper' he had seen during the war.[3]

Part of the attraction of Smuts' pamphlet lay in its compelling vision, which was strikingly expressed. Lloyd George particularly liked its conclusion, that 'mankind is once more on the move. The very foundations have been shaken and loosened ... The tents have been struck, and the great caravan of humanity is once more on the move.' Informing

Smuts' thinking was a vision of a League that would be not merely a meeting place for diplomats, but 'a great organ of the ordinary peaceful life of civilisation ... part and parcel of the common international life of states ... an ever-visible, living, working organ of the polity of civilisation.'

He proposed that such a League should be led by a Council of the five Great Powers – the United States, Britain, France, Italy and Japan – (with Germany to be admitted later) but balanced by four smaller states. There should also be a 'general conference, or congress, of all constituent states ... in which public debates of general international interest will take place'. Smuts' League included proposals for the peaceful settlement of disputes which broadly followed Phillimore lines: arbitration, conciliation and sanctions to be employed against states resorting to war without complying with the agreed procedures. He also saw disarmament as one of the League's most important functions, and suggested that the League Council should have the power to inspect all national arms factories, and that private manufacture of armaments should be abolished.

But Smuts' most interesting proposal was that the new League should serve as the 'reversionary' for the people and territories formerly belonging to Russia, Austria-Hungary and Turkey. He argued that these were now 'bankrupt estates' and that the League should become their 'liquidator or trustee'. 'Reversion to the League of Nations should be substituted for any policy of national annexation', and then the League would delegate 'authority, control or administration' to another state to act as an agent or Mandatory for the new states now emerging from the break up of the old eastern and south-eastern European order. It is ironic that Smuts never envisaged his embryo Mandates system as being suitable for use in former German colonies in Africa and the Pacific, which, he wrote, were inhabited by 'barbarians, who not only cannot possibly govern themselves, but to whom it would be impracticable to apply any idea of political self-determination in the European sense ... The disposal of these colonies should be decided on the principles which President Wilson has laid down in the fifth of his celebrated Fourteen Points.'

Smuts' pamphlet was tabled at the Imperial War Cabinet in mid-December, and when Lloyd George and the Foreign Secretary Arthur Balfour met Wilson in London on Boxing Day for a business meeting, the British Prime Minister handed him a copy. Lloyd George later recalled: 'I gave him Smuts' plan and begged him to consider it. He intimated that he did not want any assistance but, after reading Smuts' memorandum, swallowed it whole, and the League as propounded was really a British production, although fathered by President Wilson.'[4] There was considerable truth in this comment. Wilson was indeed very struck by Smuts' League vision, and many elements of it found their way into Wilson's first Paris draft of a League Covenant drawn up in early January, including a Council with four smaller powers alongside the Great Powers, and the proposals for a Mandates system, extended to cover not just eastern and south-eastern European states but German colonies as well.

Inevitably, however, while Wilson incorporated the Phillimore proposals for the peaceful settlement of disputes into his scheme, it also contained his cherished clause outlining the guarantees of territorial integrity and political independence which member states would agree to uphold, an undertaking conspicuously lacking from all British League schemes. On 19 January 1919, Wilson showed his scheme to

Lord Robert Cecil who confided to his diary: 'It is almost entirely Smuts and Phillimore combined, with practically no new ideas in it.'[5]

Lord Robert Cecil, like Smuts, was keen to work closely with his United States counterparts in the preparatory work for the construction of a League. Though he had resigned from the British government in November 1918, over proposals for the disestablishment of the Welsh church and because of a growing personal antipathy towards Lloyd George, he was invited by Balfour, his former boss in the Foreign Office, to take charge of Britain's League of Nations team of officials preparing for the conference. Thus he was included in Britain's delegation to Paris, though as he explained to *The Times* journalist Wickham Steed at the end of January, his position was an awkward one, 'a kind of hybrid between a minister and an official', with the consequence that 'I did not attend any of the meetings unless I was specially summoned.'[6] Nonetheless, he made it his business to keep in close touch with Colonel House and with Wilson's legal advisor, David Hunter Miller, and to make sure that the Americans had a copy of the British draft proposals for a League which he had drawn up with the help of his Foreign Office officials at the end of 1918.

The draft British scheme incorporated Foreign Office thinking on the importance of the League operating as a standing inter-state conference, with its own permanent secretariat, and with its Council providing the means for the Great Powers of the world to work together on a regular basis to maintain peace. It contained the Phillimore provisions for the peaceful settlement of disputes and combined these with a guarantee to be entered into by all members that they would work to ensure peace and restrain any resort to violence – a rather more flexible provision than Wilson's guarantees. The scheme also included separate representation at the conference for the Dominions and for India.

Throughout January, Cecil worked with Hunter Miller to align British and American thinking on the League by bringing their draft schemes as close together as possible. Both men faced problems from within their delegations. Lloyd George and Maurice Hankey, the influential secretary to the British delegation, were happy to let Cecil take the lead on League of Nations discussions, but believed that a League had most chance of success if it took shape at the end of the peace negotiations in the form of the 25 existing Allied and Associated Powers represented at Paris, and then gradually expanded as it tackled the inevitable post-war problems that would arise. They made their views clear to Cecil in a meeting at the end of January, but by this time Cecil's discussions with Miller had moved well beyond such a conception, and Cecil also knew how unshakeable was Wilson's belief that the League Covenant should be an integral element of the peace treaties. Indeed, the week previously, on 25 January, a plenary session of the Peace Conference had appointed a commission to draw up a League of Nations plan to create a League 'as an integral part of the General Treaty of Peace ... open to every civilised nation which can be relied upon to promote its objects', thus acceding to Wilson's demand that the construction of a League should be the first major task of the peace conference.

Cecil decided to ignore the strong objections which Lloyd George and Hankey held in relation to the League in the form in which it emerged from his discussions with Miller, though he acknowledged in his diary for 31 January the views of the influential British intelligence agent William Wiseman that his thinking on the League went 'a good deal further than the

Prime Minister', and had serious implications for the future. Hankey was adamant that the League project was no longer proceeding 'on sound lines' and warned the British Prime Minister that 'an acutely difficult situation' might be the result. Meanwhile, in the American delegation, Wilson and Miller encountered objections from Secretary of State Robert Lansing, who believed that Wilson's territorial guarantee and the sanctions of the Phillimore scheme ran counter to America's national interests and her sovereignty, contravened the Constitution, violated the Monroe Doctrine and would prove to be unacceptable to the Senate. He suggested that the difficulties could be overcome by adopting what he called a 'negative guarantee' whereby nations agreed not to violate the territory or political independence of other members of the League. House and Miller, sensing future political difficulties with the Senate, agreed, but Wilson himself refused to compromise and simply ignored Lansing's objections.[7]

While American and British officials worked to construct an agreed draft League constitution, the French delegation, according to Cecil, 'did not believe in the League and took no interest whatever in it except as it might bear on the question of French military security'.[8] On 22 January, his diary recorded 'the obvious disbelief of all the French in the League of Nations, except so far as it was a cloak for a perpetuation of the alliance between Britain and France to dominate the world'. Marshal Foch believed that 'it was a queer Anglo-Saxon fancy, not likely to be of the slightest importance in practice, but he recognised that his strange Allies must be humoured in matters of this kind'.[9]

The result of such marked French scepticism towards Wilson's pet project was that when the League Commission convened for its first meeting on 3 February, the text it had before it was a draft hammered together by Hunter Miller and the British legal advisor Cecil Hurst two days previously, with no French translation immediately available. Wilson, who insisted on chairing the Commission, favoured his own most recent draft scheme as the basis for negotiation, but House persuaded him that this would risk alienating Cecil who 'was the only man connected with the British Government who really had the League of Nations at heart'.[10] Thus the League Commission could either accept or amend the clauses of the Hurst-Miller draft, and inevitably the resulting draft covenant very strongly reflected its American–British parentage.

The League Commission worked intensively from 3 to 13 February, holding ten three-hour meetings in House's rooms at the Hotel Crillon, all except the last chaired by Wilson. He and House represented the United States, Cecil and Smuts represented Great Britain, Leon Bourgeois and an international lawyer, Ferdinand Larnaude, were the French representatives, the Italian Prime Minister Vittorio Orlando and a lawyer and diplomat Vittorio Scialoja spoke for Italy, and the Japanese were represented by their Foreign Minister Baron Makino and Ambassador to Britain, Viscount Chinda. In addition to Great Power representation, the Commission also started with five representatives of smaller powers, Paul Hymans, Belgium's Foreign Minister, Wellington Koo from China, Epitácio Pessoa of Brazil, Jayme Batalha Reis from Portugal and a Serbian representative, Milenko Vesnić. At the first meeting, these five representatives protested at what they saw as the over-representation of the Great Powers, and with French and Italian support, in the face of British and American opposition, they succeeded in expanding smaller power representation by a further four, with Eleftherios Venizelos, Prime Minister of Greece, Roman Dmowski, head of the Polish National Council, Karl Kramar, the Prime Minister of Czechoslovakia and a Romanian diplomat Constantin Diamandy, subsequently joining the Commission at its fifth meeting.

Wilson proved to be a very adept, businesslike chairman and kept discussions moving, despite the need for frequent translations from English to French to help the non-English speaking members of the Commission. Miller, who was present taking verbatim notes which were subsequently published, recorded in his diary that the American President 'dominated the League of Nations Commission meetings' though his deputy, Cecil, 'had also great influence' because of his 'long experience' and 'his patience and his willingness to listen to argument'. Nonetheless, the two men did not have things all their own way. They were challenged on some issues by the combined weight of the representatives of the smaller powers, on others by repeated French demands for more stringent League powers and by Japanese demands for the inclusion of a racial equality clause. And in discussions on Wilson's political and territorial guarantees, they found themselves inevitably on opposite sides of the argument.

After increasing the representation of the smaller powers on the Commission, their delegates pushed for four representatives of smaller powers on the League Council itself. Smuts and Wilson had earlier suggested this but it was omitted from the Hurst-Miller draft because Cecil insisted that the League could only work effectively if it was driven by a Council representing the Great Powers, meeting regularly to deal with problems and to resolve disputes. Despite the best efforts of Wilson and Cecil, nine delegates voted in favour of the admission of the lesser powers to the Council, and none against. Cecil tried vainly to recover the ground lost, strongly advising 'going slow on the proposal to give the smaller powers four representatives on the Council. Our purpose is ... to make the League a success, and that demands the support of the Great Powers. Two representatives of the lesser powers should suffice'. Whereupon Hymans protested vehemently: 'What you propose is a revival of the Holy Alliance of unhallowed memory.' The smaller powers stood firm, and, with the backing of the French and Italian delegates, finally secured agreement on 13 February that there would be four smaller powers on the League Council.[11] Cecil did defeat Hymans over the location of the League's headquarters when Geneva, not Brussels, was chosen. Britain favoured Geneva because it was not a capital city and was situated in a small, neutral country.

Battle was now joined on Wilson's proposed guarantees of territorial integrity and political independence. For Wilson, these were fundamental to his concept of a League, as he explained: '... There must be a provision that we mean business and not discussion. This idea, not necessarily these words, is the key to the whole Covenant ...' But the British delegates adamantly opposed what they saw as an inflexible provision to uphold the *status quo*. While Smuts argued that it went 'further than anything else in the document', Cecil feared the extent of the obligation 'which means war if it means anything'. He warned Wilson that 'things are being put in which cannot be carried out literally and in all respects'. The British representatives were alone in their protests, though they did persuade Wilson to propose an amendment that in the event of aggression 'the Executive Council shall advise the plan and the means by which this obligation shall be fulfilled'. This clause undoubtedly softened the impact of the guarantee scheme which would now only take effect if all League Council members were in agreement, but it increased the antagonism of Lloyd George and Hankey to the emerging League.[12]

Cecil tried to qualify the guarantee further by proposing to permit the League to 'make provision for the periodic revision of treaties which have become obsolete'. Although he failed to add this to the guarantee clause itself, he did achieve the insertion of a separate article granting League members the right to 'advise the reconsideration ... of treaties which have become inapplicable and the consideration of international conditions whose continuance might endanger the peace of the world'. This later became Article 19 of the League Covenant.[13]

The French delegates now unleashed their demands for two additional provisions, without which they argued that the League would have no real power: the establishment of an international General Staff to prepare and keep up to date the military and naval measures necessary to ensure the speedy enforcement of the obligations of the Covenant, and of a Permanent Commission to oversee members' armaments and armament programmes, including 'industries susceptible of being adapted for war purposes'. As Bourgeois emphasised to Wilson, France believed that: 'Without military backing in some force, and always ready to act, our League and our Covenant will be filed away, not as a solemn treaty, but simply as a rather ornate piece of literature.'[14] Wilson's response was that, for the United States, such an approach would be 'unconstitutional and also impossible'. Undaunted, Bourgeois tried again, only to be told by Wilson that 'no country would accept an international General Staff which would have the right to interfere with its own naval and military plans'. The French amendment was rejected by 12 votes to 3, but to try to appease Bourgeois and Larnaude, an article was added to provide for a Permanent Commission which would 'advise the League on the execution of the stipulations' of the article on disarmament, 'and in general on military and naval questions'. Despite their defeat, the two French delegates had achieved one of Clemenceau's main objectives, to demonstrate the powerlessness of the League to guarantee French security, thus enabling him 'to demand extra guarantees on the Rhine'. Cecil, in a blunt warning to the French delegates, told them that the League of Nations would be 'their only means of getting the assistance of America and England, and if they destroyed it they would be left without an ally in the world'.[15] Such threats had no impact on Clemenceau, who continued to press the case that French security could only be guaranteed by alliances with Britain and the United States, not by the embryo league.

The French had more success in ensuring that no nation could be admitted to the League 'unless it has representative institutions which permit of its being considered as itself responsible for the acts of its own Government; unless it is in a position to give effective guarantees of its sincere intention to abide by its agreement; and unless it conforms to those principles which the League shall formulate regarding naval and military forces and armaments'. This was an attempt to exclude Germany from the League unless and until she was thoroughly democratised and disarmed. The League Commission accepted these French provisions governing admission of new members.[16] Cecil, meanwhile, secured Wilson's agreement that the British Dominions and India should become founder members of the League in their own right.

While Wilson managed to head off French attempts to provide the League with military forces, and sidelined the scheme for a League which the Italian delegates proposed, he faced one final challenge to the Hurst-Miller draft during this first intensive phase of meetings. The two Japanese delegates, who had been fairly quiet members of the Commission, wanted a clause upholding the principle of racial equality, arguing this would be a parallel provision to Wilson's clause setting out the principle of religious equality. Such a clause was likely to arouse strong emotions when many countries, including the United States and Australia, operated policies openly discriminating against immigrants from Asian countries. Wilson's first response was to reject the Japanese proposal, simultaneously omitting the religious equality provision from the draft. However, the Japanese delegates persisted, raising it again two months later during the second round of meetings of the League Commission. Despite the fact that 11 out of 19 of the Commission's members supported the proposal, Wilson reiterated the 'serious objections' of some delegates, and declared the amendment not carried.[17]

The Hurst-Miller draft Covenant emerged from the first round of the meetings of the League Commission relatively unscathed, and the resulting League constitution was read out clause by clause to a plenary Conference session on 14 February. Wilson proudly declared 'a living thing is born', telling delegates that 'throughout this instrument we are depending primarily and chiefly upon ... the moral force of the public opinion of the world ... if the moral force of the world will not suffice, the physical force of the world shall. But that is the last resort because this is intended as a constitution of peace, not as a League of War.' Bourgeois' interpretation was, not surprisingly, rather different. He pointed out that the Commission took into account 'the geographical situation and the circumstances of each country' in the determination which would be made 'of the armaments of each state ... where some frontiers are exposed to greater dangers than others, it will be permissible for a state thus placed at a dangerous spot to fortify itself more strongly and to increase its army strength and its armaments'. Cecil, for his part, echoed the Phillimore Committee's view that 'no nation shall go to war with any other nation until every other possible means of settling the dispute shall have been fully and fairly tried' and expressed the strong belief of the British government that 'if we can once get the nations of the world into the habit of co-operating with one another, you will have struck a great blow at the source and origin of all or almost all the world wars which have defaced the history of the world'.[18]

Immediately after this plenary session, Wilson left Paris to return to the United States to prepare for a new session of Congress. In Washington, he encountered growing opposition amongst his political opponents to his Peace Conference diplomacy and particularly to the emerging Covenant. Particularly serious was a declaration supported in the Senate on 3 March by more than a third of its members that the constitution of the League 'as now proposed' was unacceptable to the United States. These senators urged that the settlement with Germany should be completed before further consideration was given to the League project. On his return to Paris in mid-March, Wilson knew he must seek changes in the draft Covenant to make it more palatable to Congress, particularly the Senate.

In Britain, meanwhile, the embryo League was being denounced in Labour and radical circles as a new and reactionary 'Holy Alliance' rather than a league of peoples offering hope for the future. Right-wing critics and the War Office and Admiralty, on the other hand, warned that it would not be able for many years to provide the level of security that Britain drew from its navy and empire, and that membership must not weaken Britain's world power status. More positively, Hankey thought the draft Covenant was 'infinitely better' than earlier drafts. Nevertheless, Lloyd George felt obliged to warn the House of Commons on 12 February that differences of opinion remained 'with regard to its functions and the extent to which it ought to have the power of committing great nations to war'. In Paris, the Canadian delegation was so seriously concerned about the scale of obligations which Wilson's guarantee clause might entail that it suggested to the British Empire Delegation on 13 March that it 'should be struck out or materially amended'.[19]

The League Commission reconvened on 22 March with Wilson suggesting a number of additional provisions: most notably a clause clarifying that disputes arising from a member's 'domestic jurisdiction' lay outside the legal competence of the League; that no member could be required to go to war in defence of the Covenant against the provisions of its own constitution; and a provision enabling a state to withdraw from League membership by giving two years' notice of its intentions. Wilson also proposed a clause to 'safeguard' the special status of regional understandings such as the Monroe Doctrine.

As the Peace Conference moved into its final, fraught weeks, the Big Four, soon reduced to Three as the Italians stormed out, became deadlocked over a range of intractable issues. The League project inevitably got caught up in the resulting acrimony, as Clemenceau held out for a military undertaking from Britain and from the United States, the Italians fought to secure Fiume and other territorial concessions in the Adriatic, and Lloyd George tried to put pressure on Wilson and House 'to give up their plan of building ships against Britain'.[20] On 6 April, Wilson threatened to leave the Conference, and as Cecil noted in his diary, this was a serious challenge to the Allied leaders since 'as the conference goes on the dominating position of America becomes more and more evident. The great want of the future is money, and the only one of the associated Governments that has money at its command is the United States.'[21] In the end, compromises were finally hammered out and, as a result, Clemenceau and Lloyd George agreed that the League constitution should indeed become an integral part of the peace settlement.

Once more the League Commission met, on 10 April, to finish its work. Behind the scenes, Miller and Cecil agreed that Belgium, Brazil, Spain and Greece would be the first four small states to be proposed for League Council membership. As Miller noted in his diary on 20 April: 'We thought that Belgium and Brazil were more or less inevitable; ... Spain was the largest neutral ... and ... Greece was the best of the Balkan States. I thought that perhaps it should be China instead of Greece but was convinced on this point by the thought that for the present one Asiatic Power is enough ...'[22] Meanwhile, Hankey had been informally offered, and turned down, the position of Secretary-General to the League, unhappy with the way the new body was being shaped, concerned that Senate opposition to the League in the United States would scupper United States membership and convinced that he could play a more important role by continuing in his present role. As he wrote to his wife on 18 April, 'the British Empire is worth a thousand Leagues of Nations ... I can do more for the peace of the world [in London] than in Geneva'. In his place, a rising star in the British Foreign

Office, Eric Drummond, described by the British Secretary of State for India Edwin Montagu as 'the best private secretary ever known', accepted the post.[23]

On 28 April the Plenary Conference unanimously adopted the League Covenant, though without the euphoria which had attended the appearance of the draft Covenant on 14 February. By this stage of the Conference, many delegates and officials present had become seriously disillusioned by the incessant bargaining entailed in hammering out a series of peace treaties. For some members of the British delegation, including Cecil, Smuts and the economist John Maynard Keynes, Germany was being treated too harshly, while their French counterparts thought the treaty would be too lenient to contain a resurgence of German power within a few years. Such fears were compounded by growing uncertainty over the United States. Would Wilson be able to persuade his countrymen to ratify the peace settlement and take up membership of the League of Nations? How could the settlement be made to work, and of what value would the League be without the United States on board?

The League, as it finally emerged at the end of April, was a complex organisation resulting from a series of compromises, chiefly struck between Wilson, House and Miller on the American side and Cecil, Smuts and British Foreign Office officials. Its scope was potentially wide-ranging, and it was equipped to carry out a variety of different roles which, singly or in combination, it was hoped. would preserve international peace.

First and foremost, it was to operate as a standing international conference, a body which would meet regularly and be ready to settle conflicts before they escalated out of control. It was to operate through a periodic Assembly of all member states, and a Council which was to meet at least once a year and which was designed to be the main engine of the League, with its Great Power members as the principal drivers. A permanent secretariat in Geneva would service the new organisation.

It was strongly believed, particularly in Britain, that had such a body existed in the summer of 1914, the First World War would not have broken out. As Lloyd George reminded a cabinet meeting on 24 December 1918, in July of 1914 'Lord Grey proposed a conference; Germany refused. If there had been in existence a regular permanent machinery, Germany could not have refused a summons to attend. The meeting would have been automatic. Could anyone imagine in those circumstances that the dispute would not have been settled'?[24] One of the greatest ironies of the inter-war period was that the League of Nations was carefully designed to prevent the First World War from breaking out again; as a *Daily News* editorial of 3 August 1922 stated, it was established to 'prevent a repetition of the debacle of 1914'. Its machinery was aimed at limiting conflict, not preventing it altogether, and was based on relatively optimistic assumptions about the orderly and rational conduct of democratic governments.

The intention was to contain aggression and to allow time for peaceful solutions to disputes to be sought; but there was already clear recognition in 1919 that this might not always be feasible. A British press statement in Paris on 28 April emphasised that the League had to depend on 'the free consent, in the last resort, of its component states'. If nations continued to be bellicose, 'no institution or machinery will restrain them'. Balfour's prescient warning a few years later, that 'the danger I see in the future is that some powerful nation will pursue a realpolitik in the future as in the past …

I do not believe we have yet found, or can find, a perfect guarantee against this calamity', perfectly epitomised the views of his government colleagues and officials. No machinery in the world could stop an aggressor who really meant business, but at least a League which met regularly could endeavour to prevent large numbers of other nations from being dragged into the resulting conflict.[25]

The League's second major role was to promote disarmament. Many blamed a spiralling arms race, encouraged by private cartels of armament manufacturers, for the debacle of 1914. They shared Grey's belief that 'great armaments lead inevitably to war ... the enormous growth of armaments in Europe, the sense of insecurity and fear caused by them – it was these that made war inevitable'. As George Barnes, a Labour member of Lloyd George's coalition government, told the plenary session of the Peace Conference on 14 February: 'If there be an excess of guns, there will always be a chance of getting them fired off.' The League's task was to prevent a spiralling future arms race, and ensure that there was no excess of guns to be fired off.[26]

Britain saw League-sponsored schemes of arms limitation helping to contain naval competition from other powers. As Lloyd George urged in his late March Fontainebleau Memorandum, written to try to resolve some of the difficult issues still dividing the peacemakers, 'the leading members of the League of Nations should arrive at an understanding between themselves in regard to armaments ... The first condition of success for the League of Nations is ... a firm understanding between the British Empire and the United States of America and France and Italy that there will be no competitive building up of fleets or armies between them'. General schemes of armament limitation would also legitimise the stringent

disarming of Germany under the terms of the peace settlement. As the Allied and Associated Powers made clear to the
protesting German delegates in May 1919, German disarmament was 'the first step towards that general reduction and
limitation of armaments which they seek to bring about as
one of the most fruitful preventives of war, and which it will
be one of the first duties of the League of Nations to promote'.

The League's third major role was to ensure that its
members guaranteed each others' territorial integrity and
political independence against external aggression. For
Wilson, this set of guarantees was the most fundamental
aspect of the League, without which it would be a mere
'debating society'. His League was the opposite of 'balance
of power' politics, which had produced only 'aggression and
selfishness and war'. British peacemakers feared such an
inflexible role for the League, with its implication that 'the
frontiers of the signatory states, as they stood at the signing
of peace, were regarded as being unalterable under all circumstances'. It was one thing for a country with the economic, military and political strength of the United States
to guarantee frontiers in Central and South America; it was
quite another to impose such an extensive obligation on all
League members at a time when large areas of Europe and
the Middle East were still in a state of extreme flux. In this
role, the League was cast as the guarantor of the peace treaties, which pleased the French delegates and those from the
new states of eastern and south-eastern Europe, but alarmed
Smuts and Cecil, who feared that the Treaty of Versailles, in
particular, 'may be an unsound basis on which to erect the
League'.[27]

A Liberal friend of the *Manchester Guardian* editor, C P
Scott, wrote to him in May 1919 that 'the League of Nations

as formed to guarantee this settlement seems to be not an imperfect good thing but a definitely bad thing like the Holy Alliance ...'. And Dominion leaders, viewing the trouble spots of Europe from afar, were equally convinced of the dangers of Wilson's guarantee scheme. As the Canadian delegates protested to Cecil in April: 'The proposal constituted in effect a system of mutual insurance, but was it fair to place the same liability upon all? The risks to which different members of the League were subject were by no means equal. In Canada, for instance, the risk of invasion was remote, while in France or in some Balkan states it might be great.'[28]

British delegates tried hard, with some success, to soften the impact of the guarantee provision, and to facilitate a process of peaceful change. There was also a provision in the Covenant enabling members to bring to the attention of the League disputes in which they were not themselves directly involved, but which they believed might threaten to disturb international peace. The League could then take appropriate action to deal with the problem. Thus a fourth role of the League was to try to prevent conflicts from breaking out by revising treaties, or by taking prompt and preventive measures to resolve differences between states.

As Wilson confided to his wife towards the end of the peace negotiations at Paris, where the peace settlements needed fixing 'one by one the mistakes can be brought to the League for readjustment, and the League will act as a permanent clearing house where every nation can come, the small as well as the great'.[29] Lloyd George emphasised this aspect of the League's role as British criticisms of the Treaty of Versailles mounted. He told the House of Commons in April that 'we are setting up machinery capable of readjusting and correcting mistakes'. In July he stressed its vital role to 'remedy ... repair and ... redress – the League of Nations will be there as a Court of Appeal to readjust crudities, irregularities, injustices'.[30]

If the League failed to prevent conflict from breaking out, its fifth major role was to try to secure a peaceful outcome by ensuring that members submitted disputes to be dealt with either by the League's machinery for conciliation or by arbitration, or, at the worst, to localise the fighting. In the case of disputes deemed suitable for arbitration, a permanent Court of International Justice was to be established, based at the Hague, and a panel of distinguished judges, chosen for their expertise in international law, would be able to furnish a legal opinion. Disputes deemed to be 'non-justiciable' would be considered by League Council members. This part of the League's role was based firmly on the original Phillimore Committee recommendations, designed to compel states to submit their disputes to the League, by threatening them with economic or military sanctions if they refused.

But the League's role was a limited one – it was to consider the dispute and try to resolve it, but if there was no unanimous agreement amongst League members on the rights and wrongs of the case, the country submitting the dispute could wait for three months and then strike against an adversary, without fear of any League reprisals. This reflected the thinking of British Foreign Office officials that not all wars could be prevented, but it was possible to propose machinery that would at least 'delay the outbreak of war, and secure full and open discussion of the causes of the quarrel'.

Philip Kerr, an advisor to Lloyd George at the Paris Peace Conference, believed that 'if adequate delay can really be secured after notification of a dispute likely to lead to war, the greatest menace to the general peace of the world will have been removed'.[31] The enforced delay, it was assumed, would allow tempers to cool, states who had embroiled themselves in potentially dangerous situations to extricate themselves without too much loss of face, and the League Council time to establish the facts of the conflict and to draw up a report. Finally, it would allow public opinion in the countries involved, and in all member states, to bring its pressure to bear on the leaders and governments involved in the dispute to settle it peacefully.

Securing delay, letting tempers cool, and allowing public opinion to exert its pressure in favour of peaceful settlement were seen as the key elements to enable the League to contain the outbreak of wars in the future. As Cecil told the House of Commons in July 1919, 'the great weapon we rely on is public opinion, and if we are wrong about it, the whole thing is wrong. When ... questions come up before the Council, they will be discussed and considered in public, and when, as a result of that discussion, it appears clear that one side is right and the other side is wrong, you will get the whole weight of public opinion behind the one side, and you will find ... that the nation that is in the wrong will not persist in the course which has been publicly and overwhelmingly condemned ...' Alas, the events of the next 20 years were to show that resolving disputes could not be so clear-cut, that public opinion could often inflame rather than dampen crises, and that Great Powers could view potential conflicts, and the ways in which their own interests might be affected, in very different ways.

Sanctions too, if they had to be used, were not to prove as straightforward as was envisaged in 1919, when the Allied wartime blockade had seemingly demonstrated how effective concerted economic action could be. The French delegates, very aware of what they saw as the 'gaps' in the Phillimore proposals which would allow war to be waged legally in certain circumstances, had tried to equip the League with stronger military powers to deal with aggressive states, but won no support from American or British colleagues. But their reading of the events of the previous 50 years suggested that only the prospect of an international force ready to wage war would prevent a future invasion of France by Germany.

Disputes arising from issues which, under international law, lay 'solely within the domestic jurisdiction' of a contending party were to be regarded as internal matters which could not be dealt with by the League, and this was seen by many as another gaping hole in the League's machinery to deal with conflict. However, there was one set of issues which, although domestic, was regarded as a potentially dangerous source of conflict and was specifically entrusted to the new League – the protection of the rights of racial, religious and linguistic minorities in Eastern and Central Europe. As part of the overall peace settlement, the newly-created states in these areas and all the defeated countries except Germany were to sign agreements to grant fair and equal treatment to their minority populations, which the League was to supervise. The League was thus given the onerous task of policing the internal policies adopted in these states and of trying to deal with a range of potentially endless and highly contentious disputes between governments and their ethnic minorities.

The negotiators at Paris had also turned to the League to help them to resolve three further areas of political difficulty. The Saar Basin, rich in coal, was coveted by the French, but both Lloyd George and Wilson resisted its incorporation into France, and fought successfully to place it under the authority of the League for 15 years, after which time its population could decide by plebiscite what should happen to the area. Danzig, which the Poles wished to include in their new state, was constituted as a Free City under the protection of the League, with a Commissioner to be appointed by the League. Finally, the ex-German colonies and the ex-Turkish territories, which were the subject of much heated debate in the Council of Ten in January 1919 – a body consisting of the leaders of the United States, Britain, France, and Italy with their Foreign Ministers plus two Japanese representatives – were to be constituted as Mandated areas to be administered by designated Mandatory Powers who would report annually on their stewardship to the League. Article 22 of the League Covenant laid out a detailed Mandates scheme which was to operate on the basis that the 'well being and development' of the population in the Mandated areas formed a 'sacred trust of civilisation' which the League would oversee.

The League was also charged with more general tasks; to 'secure and maintain fair and humane conditions of labour'; to supervise agreements concerning the international trafficking of women and children, and of opium and other dangerous drugs; to try to control the international trade in arms and ammunition; to bring about freedom of communications and transit and secure equitable treatment for the commerce of all members; and to take steps to prevent and control disease. A Commission on International Labour worked away in 1919 to establish an International Labour Organisation which would set international standards on working conditions and operate alongside the League. And as if that were not enough, the League was to take over the running of all 'international bureaux already established by general treaties' if the parties to the treaties consented, and to encourage and promote the establishment and co-operation of voluntary national Red Cross organisations.

Thus the League of Nations, as constituted in 1919, was a body with a broad range of functions, deliberately constructed to offer a number of different 'avenues of escape' from war. It was also to have a broad membership – 32 Allied and Associated Powers from the Peace Conference, including the British Dominions as individual members in their own right, and a number of invited powers including European countries who had been neutral in the First World War, South American countries who had been at war with Germany, and Persia. It was agreed that for the future, 'any fully self-governing State, Dominion or Colony ... may become a member of the League if its admission is agreed to by two thirds of the Assembly', provided it was willing to give guarantees of its willingness to observe international obligations and accept League regulations relating to levels of armament. But for the present, no ex-enemy country was to be allowed to join the League.

The League was therefore the world's first truly global international organisation. Its members were drawn from all five continents, and it was anticipated that eventually all the nations of the world would take up membership. But would such a diverse membership be a strength or a weakness? Council or Assembly decisions were, for the most part, to require the agreement of all members represented at the meeting; the League, in Cecil's words, was to operate with the 'least possible interference with national sovereignty'.[32] But the prospect of securing unanimous agreement to pursue specified courses of action amongst 50 or more nations would be extremely difficult, and would certainly limit the scope of League activity. That was why the British government laid so much stress on the important role of the Great Powers meeting together in the Council and giving a strong lead. But as we shall see in the next chapter, Britain, France, Italy and Japan had very different perceptions of the peace settlement, very different interests they wished to pursue, and indeed in many areas of the world were locked in fierce competition for resources, trade, and territorial and military or naval advantage. In the United States, a battle was about to be waged in the Senate over whether the country would accept the responsibilities of League membership with all the involvement in European affairs which this would inevitably entail. And in Russia, a civil war was being fought, the outcome of which would add enormously to growing international division and tension. The immediate prospects for the new organisation were not very encouraging.

3

A Faltering Start

When the plenary Peace Conference adopted the League Covenant on 28 April 1919, it was widely assumed that the first League Assembly would meet in the autumn, possibly in Washington. Though the Covenant could have no legal force until the Peace Treaty was ratified, this was not expected to be a lengthy process. However, when the Treaty of Versailles was finally handed to the Germans, it was denounced as hypocritical and profoundly unjust, and as a betrayal of Wilson's Fourteen Points. Amongst other complaints, German leaders protested both that they had not been able to contribute to the drafting of the Covenant and that Germany should be a full League member from the outset.

The point at which Germany might join the League was an early issue for dispute amongst the peacemakers. Britain supported early German membership whilst Wilson and Clemenceau opposed it. Wilson wanted proof of an effective democratic system operating in Germany, and Clemenceau sought evidence of German good faith in international relations and in the execution of the Treaty. They had not resolved their differences by 28 June, and meanwhile events elsewhere also impeded the League's birth. Italian leaders were seriously disaffected with the settlement, claiming that their allies, especially the United States, had cheated Italy of territorial gains in the Adriatic, in the Near East and in Africa to which her participation in the war had entitled her. The militant nationalist Gabrielle D'Annunzio attacked the settlement as a 'mutilated peace' and leaders of different nationalist factions vied with each other to denounce the peacemakers' efforts. In September 1919, D'Annunzio marched into Fiume, the Adriatic seaport which had been assigned by the peacemakers to the new Serbo-Croat-Slovene state (which later became Yugoslavia) at the head of a collection of 2,000 army mutineers and nationalist supporters, and remained there for 15 months, in defiance of the Italian government, the peacemakers and the new League of Nations.

Meanwhile in the Far East, Japan, the world's newest 'Great Power', was busy trying to consolidate the extensive territorial and economic concessions, mainly on the Chinese mainland, which had been seized from Germany during the war and assigned to Japan as part of the overall peace settlement. However, Japanese expansion in China was strongly resisted by the Chinese authorities, who had been looking to Wilson to protect them against their newly-powerful neighbour. The 'May 4' movement mounted by Chinese students and intellectuals against Japan and against the terms of the peace settlement triggered mass unrest and economic boycotts throughout the major centres of eastern China. Chinese anger at what they saw as Wilson's betrayal of their cause in Paris was one of many issues which exercised United States senators as they began to scrutinise the Covenant of the League of Nations and the rest of the clauses of the Treaty of Versailles in July 1919.

Under the American constitution responsibility for rati-fying the peace settlement lay with the Senate, where since November 1918 there had been a small Republican majority. Unfortunately President Wilson had done little to keep his Republican opponents informed about the peace negotia-tions in Paris or to consult them during the drafting of the League Covenant. The Senate's Foreign Relations Commit-tee, which was entrusted with the detailed examination of the Treaty of Versailles, was chaired by Henry Cabot Lodge, a fierce political opponent of Wilson, who strongly disliked both the President and his peace programme. From mid-July, the Foreign Relations Committee began a detailed considera-tion of the Treaty of Versailles and called witnesses to give evidence, many of them extremely hostile to the prospect of American membership of the League. Senators started to draw up lists of reservations which could accompany United States ratification of the Treaty and safeguard America's freedom of action as a League member.

In a bid to move the debate from Capitol Hill and take it to the American people, Wilson set off on 3 September on an 8,000-mile speaking tour of the country to sell the peace settlement and in particular his vision of the role of the League of Nations in preserving the future peace of the world. Audiences were receptive, but on 25 September, in Colorado, Wilson collapsed from the strain, and was rushed back to Washington, where on 2 October he suffered a near-fatal stroke. From that time onwards, he was confined to his rooms at the White House, partially paralysed but ever more desperate to ensure that Democratic Senators rejected any attempt by Republicans to attach reservations to American membership of the League.

Events in the United States were viewed with growing

alarm in Britain and France. Both Lloyd George and Clemenceau had modified their treaty demands at Paris to ensure that the United States would take a full part in upholding the settlement. Clemenceau had given up his fight for the Rhine to be the frontier between France and Germany in return for guarantees of assistance against aggression from the United States and Britain. Now American accession to the treaty and participation in the League was becoming increasingly uncertain. But could Britain and France between them enforce the peace on Germany and operate an effective League of Nations? Lord Bryce, a former Ambassador to the United States, was not alone in the view which he expressed to Smuts in summer 1919 that 'without the United States, the whole thing will fail'.[1] Lloyd George was becoming seriously worried about the consequences of American non-participation in the League. As his foreign policy advisor Philip Kerr confided to the legal advisor at the Foreign Office, Cecil Hurst, the question that was exercising Lloyd George's mind at present 'is that the Covenant of the League of Nations imposes considerable obligations upon all the members, particularly upon the Great Powers and most of all upon the British Empire with its worldwide interests. The one element which made the representatives of the Great Powers at Paris accept the scheme without exhaustive consideration of the obligations which the League would entail was the fact that all the nations of the world and especially all the Five Great Powers would be, so to speak, in the same boat and would share the burden in common. Consequently, any modification of the obligations entered into by any one of the Five Great Powers or any failure of any one of the Five to ratify the Treaty modifies the situation profoundly and if there is a chance of the United States not becoming a member of the

League at all or becoming a member upon terms which will place it in a position substantially different from those of the other members, the question of the British Empire undertaking these obligations at all ought to be considered very carefully.'[2]

Clearly, Lloyd George could not intervene directly in the American political process, but pending the appointment of a new Ambassador to the United States, the British government despatched Lord Grey, the former Liberal Foreign Secretary, to the United States in mid September to hold discussions with influential State Department officials, Senators and members of the Presidential entourage in particular about naval issues and the League of Nations. Unfortunately, Grey's arrival in the United States on 27 September coincided with Wilson's collapse. As a consequence his mission achieved little of substance, and he was unable to influence events in the Senate, which by early November were reaching a bitter climax.

On 6 November Lodge proposed 14 reservations to the Treaty of Versailles, which had been broadly agreed by Republican senators. They had the effect of exempting the United States from any League obligations in relation to limitation of armaments, guarantees of territorial integrity and political independence of member states or economic or military sanctions, and would allow Congress to demand American withdrawal from the League whenever it wanted and to define unilaterally what constituted a 'domestic' issue over which the League had no jurisdiction. These far-reaching reservations were agreed by the Senate on 15 November. Four days later, the vote was taken on whether to agree to the peace treaty with the accompanying reservations. With Wilson urging Democrat Senators from his sick bed to vote against the treaty with reservations attached, enough of them heeded his call to ensure that in this form it was rejected by 55 votes to 39. But a motion to pass the treaty without any reservations was also rejected, by 53 votes to 37. While a majority of Senators were willing to join the League with some reservations attached, they could not agree on what these should be.

The news of American rejection of League membership reached London just as the British government was examining the implications of a League operating without the United States. For the British government, with its Empire of 13 million square miles and 450 million inhabitants spanning six continents, they were extremely worrying. As Hurst pointed out, 'the principle for which the Allied Powers at Paris purported to be struggling … was that of substituting the principle of sharing in common the obligations of the civilised states for the condition of affairs which had prevailed up to the time of the war of mere individual regulation of international relations. Once the principle is admitted that one or more of the great Powers is to stand outside the settlement, the inevitable result must be to reintroduce the old state of affairs with all the uneasy conditions which have prevailed in Europe for the last two decades … The United States is now so rich that no other Power could keep pace with her in a competitive struggle for armaments. For the British Empire, depending on its fleet for security, the outlook would be particularly disquieting.'

And it was not just an American naval challenge which Britain feared. There was also the serious prospect of commercial antagonism. As Hurst noted, 'To the British Empire the exclusion of the United States from the obligations under Article 10 means that burdens might have to be supported single-handedly which no Government would lightly undertake without an assurance that the other great States would do their part, more particularly its great commercial rival across the Atlantic. Great Britain cannot take part in a war without diverting its shipping and its commerce from their normal channel, and if the United States are to be free to stand out, the Americans would use the opportunity to seize trade opportunities which Great Britain was forced to forego ... The economic boycott was the weapon wherewith the League intended to coerce an aggressor or recalcitrant member ... An economic boycott with the Americans standing outside it is certain to mean that the Americans will endeavour to trade with the boycotted country.' Hurst saw no alternative but for the British government to safeguard its position by coupling its 'ratification of the Treaty with a declaration that they will withdraw from the League at the end of ... two years ... It could be made subject to an intimation that if all the other civilised Powers joined the League it would be withdrawn, and also with a suggestion that unless they had done so, a conference of all the Powers who signed the Treaty of Peace with Germany and all those who were invited to become original members of the League should take place to arrive at an agreed substitute for the existing Covenant.' Hurst's recommendation was fully supported by the Foreign Secretary, Lord Curzon, who circulated it to fellow Cabinet members and sent it to Grey in the United States, emphasising the difficulties 'that would accrue' for Britain 'if the United States fail to become a party to the Treaty or endeavoured to become a party on terms in any way approximate to those indicated in the reservations'.[3]

The Senate deadlock continued. Wilson's opponents made much of the charge that Britain and her Dominions would have six votes in the League as against only one for the United States and would therefore have an unfair advantage, glossing over the fact that all major decisions would require unanimity at least of Council members. Many Democrat Senators, who wanted to see the United States in the League, were persuaded that this could only happen if they were willing to accept at least some Republican reservations, and were angered by Wilson's continued hard-line stance of the 'treaty, the whole treaty and nothing but the treaty'. Early in 1920, the Senate Foreign Relations Committee once more drew up a list, this time of 15 reservations, which in March were accepted by the Senate. On 19 March, the peace treaty and the reservations were put to the vote, and although 49 Senators supported them, 12 hard-line Republican 'irreconcilables' and 23 Democrats who agreed with Wilson's stance were opposed. Without a two-thirds majority, the Treaty fell, taking with it any chance of American membership of the League. A further casualty of Senate rivalries was the American guarantee to France, which was repudiated without being put to a vote. Lloyd George had managed to tie a similar British guarantee to the acceptance of the obligation by the United States. Thus Britain was able to pull out of this particular agreement, but still faced the alarming prospect of League membership without the economic power and naval strength of the United States.

The British War Office had already warned the Cabinet in January 1920, that 'we cannot afford to regard America as a potential enemy, as the expenditure entailed by adequate preparations to fight her would be so vast as to be out of the question in the present state of the nation's finances ... it is imperative that our policy should be so directed as to eliminate any possibility of a rupture between the United States of America and the British Empire'.[4] The Admiralty was totally opposed to the prospect of military sanctions being employed by the League, convinced that the job of enforcing them would be assigned to the hard-pressed and dangerously-stretched British navy. With the United States now out of the League, and likely to challenge any naval blockade or attempt in a crisis to search neutral ships on the high seas, the dangers of naval action under the League's auspices were considerably increased.

Whilst events in the United States cast a long shadow over the viability of the League, the ratification of the peace settlement by the Allied powers in January 1920 was the prelude to a prolonged period of increasingly bitter arguments between Britain and France over how to enforce the Treaty terms on an antagonistic Germany. It had been agreed at the end of the Paris Peace Conference that the execution of the terms would be overseen at a strategic level by the Supreme Council, at which the Allied leaders would periodically meet to assess progress, and at an operational level by the Conference of Ambassadors, a body of Allied officials based in Paris.

For over two years, the Supreme Council met at a succession of European venues as the Allies struggled to disarm Germany and to extract reparations. They disagreed on the most appropriate tactics to use, with France favouring a punitive approach and Britain a more conciliatory stance. The one thing they did agree on, however, was that the execution of the settlement, and all issues relating to it, should be the responsibility of the Supreme Council and not the League of Nations. Whilst some officials, such as the British Cabinet Secretary Maurice Hankey, argued that this benefited the League, and that the 'Supreme Council had done the League a good turn by relieving it of the more immediate and more disagreeable aftermath of war',[5] League supporters, such as Lord Cecil, feared that 'if the Supreme Council continues side by side with the League, the latter's authority will be destroyed'.[6] Even *The Times*, on 5 May 1920, expressed concern that Lloyd George seemed intent on enlarging the Supreme Council so as to override the Council of the League and form an 'arbitrary and unauthorised "international government" with the Supreme Council becoming a semi-permanent instrument for the reconstruction of Europe'. A year later, a Cambridge Union debate approved the motion that 'it was now time for the League of Nations to supplant the Supreme Council in all matters touching the peace of the world'.[7]

However, the dilemma facing Lloyd George, as he explained it to British Dominion and colonial representatives at the 1921 Imperial Conference held in London, was that 'You cannot have a League of Nations without America; it would not be of the least use'. And as long as the Republican Party remained in power, 'they will not come in'. This had been made abundantly clear after the Republican candidate, Warren G Harding, won the Presidency by a large margin in November 1920. Cabot Lodge gloated that the Republicans had 'destroyed Mr. Wilson's League of Nations ... we have torn up Wilsonism by the roots.'.[8] How should the British Government respond? Lloyd George's mind turned to the possibility of constructing an alternative international body of a looser kind, which America might be induced to join, and was encouraged by a report from the new British Ambassador to the United States, Sir Auckland Geddes, that the United States Secretary of State Charles Evans Hughes had asked him 'if the existing League could not be turned into an organ to enforce the terms of the Treaty of Versailles, and if a new association of Nations could not be formed outside the

League. We are to discuss the matter further.'[9] There was no follow-up to this proposal, but in the autumn, Lloyd George's former Chief Whip, Freddy Guest, reported on a recent visit to the United States that 'there is a distinct turn in the tide of political thought in favour of America entering a League of Nations. Harding and Hughes are openly spoken of as being in favour of such a policy. They may find it difficult to join the present League as such, but will probably be ready to come in to some other similar international peace machinery, especially if their entrance can coincide with that of Germany.'[10]

Meanwhile the American President was pursuing a rather different course. While the United States prepared to sign a separate peace treaty with Germany, Harding issued an invitation to the world's principal naval powers in mid July to attend a conference to be held in Washington in the autumn to discuss naval limitation, Pacific and Far Eastern questions. Clearly signalling to the American people that their interests could be safeguarded most effectively by traditional diplomatic negotiations, Harding and Secretary of State Hughes dominated the Washington Conference, securing all their major objectives. The United States, Britain, Japan, Italy and France agreed on a ratio for the limitation of their capital ships, which gave the United States parity with Britain for the first time, and allowed Japan to build up to 60 per cent of United States and British capital ship strength. Japan also demanded that no new fortifications or naval bases should be built in the Pacific area and this was agreed, though with considerable bargaining about what would constitute 'the Pacific area'; Singapore was excluded, as were islands 'adjacent' to Canada, Australia and New Zealand. At American insistence, the Anglo-Japanese Alliance, dating back to 1902, was terminated and replaced by a four-power pact between the

United States, France, Britain and Japan, under which the signatories agreed to settle disputes in the Pacific by peaceful consultation. A nine-power pact was also concluded in relation to concessions on the Chinese mainland, with China, the Netherlands, Portugal and Belgium joining the five leading naval powers in agreeing to respect China's territorial integrity and political independence, renounce any further attempts to seek spheres of influence, and allow equal commercial opportunity for all. Under the auspices of the United States, direct negotiations between China and Japan resulted in the return of the Shantung Concession, seized by Japan from Germany during the war, to China. Thus the Washington Conference resulted in far-reaching agreements relating to arms limitation and peaceful settlement, negotiated independently of the League of Nations. The Republican administration had made its point loudly and clearly; the United States could safeguard its interests very effectively without incurring the onerous obligations of League membership.

Lloyd George now turned his attention to the possibility of replacing the League with a broad association of European powers which could include both Germany and Russia. Having been let down by the United States, the French government were desperately seeking to buttress their security through an alliance with the British. In early 1922 at Cannes, Lloyd George offered Aristide Briand, French Prime Minister since January 1921, a guarantee along the lines of the one which had been agreed at Paris in 1919 in return for French support for a general European association, whose members would agree not to wage war on each other. The two leaders agreed to discuss the project further at a conference to be held in Genoa in April, and to this end 1,254 delegates representing 34 countries, including Russia and Germany, were invited to participate. Apart from France, nearly all the participating European countries were represented by their Prime Ministers, in strong contrast to the lesser lights who normally attended the League's Geneva meetings.[11] But resistance to Lloyd George's scheme came from many quarters. Briand was replaced as Prime Minister by Poincaré, who refused to attend, but demanded from Britain a much more precise military undertaking than the rather loose guarantee Lloyd George had been offering and made it clear that he would oppose German and Russian membership of any existing or new international body.

Other European leaders expressed little enthusiasm for the proposed new venture, with the Dutch foreign minister telling Lloyd George that 'the Pact might tend to weaken the League of Nations, since nations which had signed it might prefer not to incur the obligations of the Covenant'. Lloyd George was prepared to be flexible, suggesting that 'the Pact of Peace should somehow be tacked on to the League of Nations' and stressing to his Dutch counterpart the importance of trying to bring America, Russia and Germany into the League.[12] Without French support and only lukewarm interest at best from powers such as Belgium and the Netherlands, however, the projected Pact could not be translated into anything concrete. Genoa instead became notorious for spawning a secret Treaty at nearby Rapallo, agreed between the European outcasts, Germany and Russia. Poincaré's worst fears were now realised, and not only would he have nothing further to do with pacts which envisaged Russian or German membership, but his resolve to keep both powers outside the League was greatly strengthened.

For the rest of 1922 and for the following year, Anglo-French relations were stormy, marked by deep personal antagonism particularly between the British Foreign Secretary Lord Curzon and Poincaré, and by serious political disagreements over events in the Near East and in Europe. And while Lloyd George had been busy seeking alternatives to the League of Nations, the French government had taken the initiative at Geneva, drawing many of the new states of eastern and south-eastern Europe into the French orbit, exploring the possibilities of different League provisions which might serve to protect French interests, and concluding alliances with Poland and Czechoslovakia which, it was hoped, would buttress French security. As Balfour had observed to Hankey in January 1921, though the French disliked the League, they had accepted the fact of its existence and 'set themselves to work to use it for all its worth'. Both the British Foreign Office and the Foreign Secretary, Curzon, urged that the British government should also now start looking to the League 'as an invaluable instrument for discharging certain duties and solving certain problems with which our machinery is not adequate to deal'.[13]

There were, indeed, an increasing number of post-war problems which the Supreme Council could not, or would not, satisfactorily resolve. Whilst it busied itself with issues arising from the execution of the peace treaties, a vast swathe of territory extending from Eastern Europe across to Russia and down to Turkey and the Near East lay beyond its control. The collapse of the Habsburg, Romanov and Ottoman Empires was followed by a series of military struggles and attempted land grabs; Estonia and Latvia fought against Russia, Lithuania against Poland, Poland against Russia, and Greece against Turkey. Armenia, Georgia and Azerbaijan declared their independence from Russia. Border disputes flared up between Persia and Russia, Hungary and

Romania, Poland and Czechoslovakia, and Italy and the new Yugoslav state. The League could assuredly help to quell some of this post-war turbulence, and in addition, the Treaty of Versailles had given it a number of specific peacekeeping responsibilities: to administer the Saar and Danzig, to supervise the protection of minorities in the new Eastern and Central European states and to oversee the administration of the Mandates system over former German overseas colonies and Turkish protectorates and provinces.

The League Council had held its first meeting in Paris on 16 January 1920, six days after the Treaty of Versailles came into force, and its second meeting was held over three days in London in February 1920. At the suggestion of the League Secretariat, the session began and ended in public, though all debate, discussion and decision-making took place behind closed doors. This second meeting laid the foundations for much of the League's future supervisory activities, establishing the outlines of the Permanent Court of International Justice, the Health Organisation, the Organisation for Communications and Transit, and the regimes which would oversee the governance of the Saar and Danzig. Consideration was also given to the procedure by which the rights of racial, religious and linguistic minority groups in Eastern and Central Europe, which had been guaranteed by a series of minority treaties drawn up at the Peace Conference, could be most effectively protected.

By the summer of 1920, the League was also being asked to deal with a number of minor but potentially inflammatory disputes. The first conflict referred to the League was by the Persian Foreign Minister, Prince Firuz, who asked for assistance to help drive Soviet Russian troops out of occupation of the Persian port of Enzeli. Given that the Persian government was already in negotiations with the Bolsheviks in Moscow to secure the withdrawal of the troops, the League decided to wait before taking any action, and the crisis passed. A more serious challenge for the League was the outbreak of hostilities between Poland and Lithuania, which started in 1920 and rumbled on for the next year or so. The dispute centred on the city of Vilna, which the Lithuanians claimed as their historic capital, but which was seized and occupied by Polish troops. Though the League Council tried hard to broker a negotiated settlement and to secure the incorporation of Vilna into the new state of Lithuania, their efforts were unsuccessful. Polish military force won the day, and the city became a part of Poland.

Hostilities also threatened to break out between Sweden and Finland in the summer of 1920 over possession of the Åland islands in the Baltic, which had been part of the Grand Duchy of Finland when it was ruled by Russia. Liberated since 1917, the islanders, who were mainly of Swedish origin, now wanted to become part of Sweden, causing serious tensions between Sweden and Finland. This was just the sort of dispute which the British government believed the League could resolve, and accordingly they referred it to the League Council in June. Given that this was the first significant test of the League's peacekeeping capabilities, the merits of the dispute were debated and considered very thoroughly, and a neutral commission was despatched to the Baltic to assess the situation and draw up a report. In 1921, the League Council accepted its recommendations that the islands should remain part of Finland, but that the League should ensure that the rights and interests of the inhabitants were not threatened in any way, and that the islands themselves should not be fortified or used as a naval base. Though neither Sweden nor

Finland were entirely happy with the outcome, they both accepted the settlement, giving the League its first major success. However, neither of these Baltic countries could be regarded as major European powers; nor did they have strong allies backing them. Future territorial conflicts, as we shall see, would not be so easily resolved.

Another crisis which was referred to the League in 1920 was the future of the newly-declared Republic of Armenia, sandwiched between Turkey and Russia, and extremely vulnerable to attack by either or both of its powerful neighbours. The Supreme Council, seeking a protector for the vulnerable new state, asked the League to agree to act as a Mandatory Power, but the League Council politely but firmly declined to take on this potentially onerous responsibility, and suggested that an individual country, possibly the United States, should be approached instead. Congress, however, rejected the proposal in June 1920, and it was left to the first League Assembly, meeting in the autumn in Geneva, to try to come up with a solution. But speeches and resolutions were of little material help to Armenia; before long, Bolshevik troops invaded and turned the country into a Soviet Republic. As Lloyd George – no friend to the League, as we have seen – remarked bitterly to his friend, the newspaper proprietor Lord Riddell in December: 'The League of Nations is, I regret to say, deceptive and dangerous. They cannot even protect a little nation like Armenia. They do nothing but pass useless resolutions.'[14]

Nevertheless, some months later in August 1921, the League proved to be a useful backstop when the Supreme Council failed to reach agreement with Germany and Poland about where the frontier between the two dividing the resource-rich region of Upper Silesia should run. A plebiscite had failed to resolve the issue; France backed Polish claims for a larger slice of the area, while Britain and Italy backed those of Germany. The League was asked to resolve the matter, and within six weeks had drawn up a line of demarcation which both Poland and Germany protestingly agreed to. Neither power accepted it as a fair or just outcome, but the dispute was now resolved, and the frontier was effectively administered under League supervision for the next 15 years.

By 1922, therefore, the League was beginning to show what it might be able to achieve. The Allies remained wary of allowing it to take on more contentious issues, however, especially those on which Britain and France were bitterly divided; the fighting between Turkey and Greece in 1922 and the resulting Chanak crisis was not referred to the League, and nor was the Franco-Belgian led invasion of the Ruhr in early 1923 or the underlying reparations issue. But the League had done enough to establish itself as a low-key but indispensable body for resolving a range of secondary but nonetheless significant problems, the latest of which – the rescue of the new Austrian Republic from economic insolvency – was referred to the League Council by the Allied powers in the autumn of 1922.

The annual League Assembly, held for representatives of all members each autumn since 1920 in Geneva's Salle de la Reformation, also helped to strengthen its influence. From the outset, the representatives of medium and smaller powers seized their opportunity to raise issues, give their view on world affairs, and put pressure on the four permanent Council members, Britain, France, Italy and Japan. Whilst no Prime Minister or Foreign Secretary of the Big Four powers visited Geneva before 1924, the Assembly gave leading government representatives of the smaller powers, working with indefatigable and dedicated architects of the League such as Lord Robert Cecil and Leon Bourgeois, considerable opportunities to hammer out agreed and efficient League processes and to establish effective ways of holding the League Council to account. By the end of 1922, after Lloyd George had fallen from power in Britain, it was the Supreme Council which went into eclipse, and the League which was left to pick up the pieces and to try to bring hope to a war-torn world.

Unfortunately, two years of acrimonious arguments between the former wartime European allies about the implementation of the peace treaties had left a bitter legacy – deep divisions and distrust between Britain and France, and the establishment in Italy of a fascist-led government under Benito Mussolini at the end of October 1922. And though most ex-enemy powers had by this time been accepted into the League, Germany remained outside, resentful and aggrieved. Soviet Russia attacked the League as a band of capitalist and imperialist powers, and the United States continued to hold itself aloof from any involvement in the League or in European disputes.

Thus the outlook for the League was far from promising. And yet the hopes of millions of people, particularly in Europe, were vested in its success. In Britain, the League of Nations Union already had 200,000 members and over half of MPs affiliated to it, all putting pressure on the British government to work through the League to bring peace to the world.[15] There were similar, though less powerful bodies, in France, Belgium, Switzerland and a host of other countries. Even Germany had its *Liga für Volkerbund* advocating German membership of the League. Democratic governments could not ignore the activities of such passionate and committed pressure groups, nor could they ignore the League.

But it remained to be seen how the leading powers would use the League to solve the post-war problems which continued to face them.

4

Conciliation or Coercion? The Development of the League in the 1920s

In the absence of the United States, it fell to Britain and France, with the help of the League Council's other two permanent members, Japan and Italy, to develop the potential of the League and to work together to build up its effectiveness in preventing and in settling international disputes. Unfortunately, however, while Italian and Japanese leaders were intent on consolidating and where possible extending their own territorial and colonial interests, Britain and France held diametrically opposing views on how to secure international peace in the aftermath of the First World War. While French leaders were obsessed with the need to secure Britain's assistance in a strict enforcement of the peace settlement to counter what they believed would be an inevitable future German bid for European supremacy, British leaders were looking to appease short-term German grievances, to assist the new Weimar regime to secure economic recovery – which would be of direct economic benefit to Britain – and to welcome her as a Great Power into the League of Nations as soon as possible. Indeed, many British political leaders in the early 1920s, including the Foreign Secretary Lord Curzon, saw French military power, rather than disarmed Germany, as the major short-term threat to the achievement of European stability. As Salvador de Madariaga, the head of the League Secretariat's Disarmament Section in the 1920s, noted so acutely, 'it is not altogether impossible to bring the French and the British to see eye to eye – only their eyes are so different'.[1]

The failure of the United States to take up League membership widened the gulf between Britain and France. While British governments were now concerned to minimise League obligations and to proceed by way of conciliation and mediation to try to resolve the myriad of post-war territorial and political disputes and to remain on cordial terms with the United States, French governments looked to the League to provide additional levels of military security and guarantees against future German aggression. Following US non-ratification of the Treaty and membership of the League, and the automatic lapsing of Britain's guarantee, which was tied to America's offer of assistance, France was left with no Rhine frontier, no prospect of American assistance against a future German attack, and no certainty of British help either. In these changed circumstances, with a declining population of 39 million (as against Germany's 66 million), with heavy war debts and facing high costs of repair for the war damage her northern industrial regions had suffered, French diplomacy now focused on the strictest possible enforcement of the Treaty of Versailles, the disarmament of Germany and her exclusion from the League for the forseeable future. This was combined with the construction of a network of East European allies, including Poland and Czechoslovakia, and the 'Little Entente' powers of Romania, Czechoslovakia and Yugoslavia, and a policy in the League of strengthening the very guarantee and sanctions articles which the British government was seeking to weaken.

Thus while British delegates at Geneva from 1920 argued consistently for a more flexible and consultative League, their French counterparts, with support from their East European allies, sought to plug what they described as alarming 'gaps' in the guarantee and sanctions articles of the Covenant, and to obtain from member states cast-iron assurances about the levels of assistance they would provide in the event of hostilities breaking out in the future. While no British government would contemplate supporting any strengthening of existing League machinery with the United States, Russia and Germany outside the League, all French governments worked to prevent any revision of treaties or serious attempts at disarmament. The result at Geneva, until the mid 1920s, was complete deadlock; all the two major powers succeeded in doing was to thwart each other's policy initiatives and to immobilise the League's peacekeeping mechanisms. As Salvador de Madariaga recalled in his memoirs, 'everything went on as if, for lack of any common adversary, France and Britain had chosen the League as the arena in which to fight each other'.[2]

We have already seen in Chapter 2 how the British Government sought to weaken Article 10 of the League Covenant, which contained the undertaking of its members to respect and to preserve each others' territorial integrity and political independence against attack, and to balance it with an additional article which would facilitate peaceful international change and the re-consideration of peace treaties after a number of years.[3] Indeed, the Canadian government had

pressed at Paris for Article 10 to be 'struck out or materially amended' but Woodrow Wilson would not countenance such a move, which he regarded as an attack on the very heart of the League itself. Nonetheless, the Canadian delegates told their fellow British Empire delegates at Paris that their objection to Article 10 was that it threw an unfair burden on countries which derived the least benefit from it, and that 'it would be Canadian policy to seek alteration of Article 10 later'.[4]

At the League Assemblies of 1920 and 1921, Canada proposed the removal of Article 10. In response, a committee of jurists examined the article intensively, and in due course reported back to the Assembly that the article merely contained 'the governing principle to which all members of the League subscribe' and that members were 'not obliged to take part in any military action'. In the light of this interpretation, Canada sought to amend Article 10 in 1922, rather than press for its removal, asking the League Council to take into account political and geographical circumstances of member states in giving their advice on how members' obligations under Article 10 should be fulfilled. Canada also sought agreement that a member should not have to engage 'in any active war without the consent of its parliament, legislature or other representative body'. In 1923, these two proposed amendments to Article 10 were submitted to the Assembly as an 'interpretive resolution', and were supported by the League's major powers, but many east European states abstained, and Persia voted against the resolution. As a result, Article 10 stayed in the Covenant, but it was clear that many League members supported Canada's flexible interpretation of the nature of members' obligations under the Article. As the chairman of the British League of Nations Union, Gilbert Murray, wrote in the *Daily News* in February 1923, 'the obligation in Article 10 is at once too widespread for any prudent nation to accept, and too vague for any prudent nation to bank upon. As the Covenant now stands, no nation would be really safe in acting on the supposition that, if it were suddenly attacked, the rest of the League would send armies to defend it.'

While the Canadians were seeking to limit the obligations that might arise under Article 10, the British government was exploring the possibilities of Article 19. Facing mounting criticism in Britain in the summer of 1919 over what seemed to many liberal-minded people to be a punitive and vindictive peace treaty, Lloyd George had made frequent references to the League's ability to 'remedy ... repair and ... redress'.[5] Within a year of the signing of the Treaty of Versailles, Curzon referred in the House of Lords to the possibility, and even the necessity at some stage, of its revision. He told his officials in the Foreign Office that 'revision will come about partly by the force of events, partly by the action of bodies such as the League of Nations to whom appeal will increasingly be addressed for its rectification'.[6] Unfortunately, however, the League's powers in this regard proved to be extremely limited. Article 19 merely allowed the League Assembly to 'advise the reconsideration by Members of the League of treaties which have become inapplicable and the consideration of international conditions whose continuance might endanger the peace of the world'.

But advice offered could, of course, be rejected, particularly if it could only be suggested and not enforced. Just as the British government sought flexibility and realism in the interpretation of Article 10, so the French government and her East European allies were unwilling to contemplate any treaty revision in Europe until they felt more secure.

And outside Europe, of course, treaty revision could have an adverse effect on the Empires and the overseas trade of both Britain and France, if it was applied to treaties such as those between Britain and Egypt, or the treaties concluded in the 19th century between European powers and the Chinese imperial government. Many League members had special interests or spheres of influence they feared could be jeopardised if Article 19 could be readily called into play, and thus early hopes of the effective operation of the Article were dashed.

It was invoked just once, by Bolivia, which had a territorial dispute with Chile in 1920. The League Assembly asked three jurists, members of the Assembly, 'to give their joint opinion on the powers of the Assembly under Article 19'. The opinion, solemnly delivered, killed off any lingering hopes about the efficacy of the Article. The collective view of the jurists was that the Assembly could only offer advice under the article 'in cases where treaties have become inapplicable- that is to say, when the state of affairs existing at the moment of their conclusion has subsequently undergone ... such radical changes that their application has ceased to be reasonably possible, or in cases of the existence of international conditions, whose continuance might endanger the peace of the world ... The Assembly would have to ascertain, if a case arose, whether one of these conditions did in point of fact exist.' Thus the Assembly could find itself in the position of having to take advice on whether it could offer advice under the article! Not surprisingly, after 1921, nothing further was heard about Article 19 at Geneva.[7]

If Articles 10 and 19 proved to be virtually impossible to enforce, how effective would the proposals be which empowered the League to resolve disputes peacefully? It was over

Articles 12 to 17, which outlined a set of rules for preventing and settling disputes, that Britain and France disagreed most strongly. On the one hand, British policy-makers did not believe that all disputes could be prevented, but that the League machinery would at least 'delay the outbreak of war and secure full and open discussion of the causes of the quarrel'. That delay would then give 'public opinion, properly organised and properly applied ... an opportunity of settling the dispute'.[8] The assumption was that delay would cool tempers rather than inflame them, that facts could be established which would show clearly that one party to a dispute was in the right and the other in the wrong, and that public opinion would exert pressure on the 'guilty' party, and not on the 'innocent' one, even if its own government was the one condemned by the League Council.

Such optimistic assumptions were not shared by the French government. Their experience over the past 50 or so years did not suggest that wars were the result of accident and misjudgement. They believed that wars were waged as part of a deliberate design by one country seeking to extend its influence, or by another in self-defence. Despite the horrifying experience of the First World War, they took the view that there would continue to be leaders who would seek to use war as an instrument of national diplomacy and who would plan to regain lost territories or expand existing ones, by armed force if necessary. French leaders had had experience of how 'facts' could be twisted; they did not believe that exhaustive investigations would result in impartial reports, and they feared that long before such reports had been compiled, let alone unanimously agreed to, a member state – probably France – could have been invaded and militarily defeated. Nor were they sanguine that, if this happened, all other League members would automatically rush to their assistance, or that international public opinion, however strongly expressed, would prevail upon the invader to withdraw. Indeed, the British government accepted that if the League Council could not agree on the merits of a dispute, the parties would be free to fight it out. This would allow a skilful national leader to disguise his hostile intentions sufficiently adroitly to hoodwink some members of the League Council, lull them into a false sense of security, and then unleash a strong military attack on another state, who would have been prevented during the previous nine months from building up military strength for fear of the Council declaring them the aggressor.

Not surprisingly, therefore, the French government was alarmed by how little protection the League was likely to offer it. Its own scheme for a League with economic and military force at its disposal had been rejected at Paris; it was now left with a set of provisions for the prevention and peaceful settlement of disputes which relegated sanctions to a subordinate position and left them flexible in operation. Therefore, after 1919 the French government worked to construct a network of alliances which would come into operation as soon as one of the parties involved was attacked, and not after the League Council had met and deliberated on how to deal with the aggression. And they demanded that the provisions of Articles 12 to 17 be tightened up, so that lack of unanimity on the part of the League Council could not prevent a solution from being enforced, and so that the sanctions outlined in Article 16 could be fully signed up to by all members, with plans drawn up to enable the League to act speedily to compel members to submit to its jurisdiction. The absence of the United States from the League made French leaders even more insistent on the importance of strengthening the machinery of the League.

As we have already seen, the effect of the withdrawal of the United States from the League had the opposite effect on British leaders – it made them believe that only a flexible and consultative League could now have any hope of operating effectively. Military and naval sanctions, unless the United States tacitly supported them, would be out of the question. The United States could well challenge a naval blockade or an attempt by a League naval force to search neutral ships on the high seas. Even economic sanctions, if effective, would run the risk of meeting military opposition. As General George Cockerill of the British War Office had pointed out already in late 1918, the use of the economic weapon would be 'wholly inconsistent with the present concept of neutrality. The adoption of such a weapon involves a relation between the nations employing it which is in reality ... an offensive and defensive alliance, an alliance of peoples ... who, having realised that international peace is their highest interest, are prepared in the last resort ... to take up arms together in its cause'.[9] There could be no doubt that the absence of the United States from the League would make the employment of such an economic weapon extremely dangerous for Britain, from both an economic and military standpoint.

British fears were shared by the Scandinavian members of the League, who were alarmed by the wording of Article 16, with its emphasis on member states undertaking to implement certain economic measures immediately upon breach of the covenants in Articles 12, 13 and 15 by an offending member state. Their wartime experience had left them feeling geographically and militarily exposed, not as a result of direct aggression against them, but through being subjected to pressures by the opposed belligerents. They wanted to reduce their obligations under the Covenant and thereby minimise their chances of being militarily threatened by being forced to take part in economic sanctions and blockades.

At the first League Assembly meeting in 1920, therefore, a Scandinavian proposal was put forward, to amend Article 16 to provide that, in the event of sanctions, members' military and geographical situations should be taken into consideration in framing the Council's recommendations, and that those states who did not vote for sanctions should not be expected to apply them. The British Government was alarmed at the potential dangers in this proposal, since it would undermine the mutual support of League members which enabled minor states to participate in an economic blockade without encountering serious risk of retaliation by powerful neighbours. On the other hand, the absence of the United States from the League made the objective of Article 16, to prevent all commercial dealings between a state which had broken the Covenant and any other state whether a member of the League or not, extremely difficult if not impossible for the League, with its current membership, to achieve.

In response to the proposal, the League Council set up an International Blockade Committee to examine the wording and consider the application of Article 16. Representatives from Britain, France, the Netherlands, Norway, Switzerland and Cuba deliberated exhaustively on the issues raised and reported back to the 1921 Assembly. Their report acknowledged that a very rigid application of Article 16 might place League members in very difficult situations. It therefore proposed graduated economic sanctions, increasing in severity if the offending state remained recalcitrant, and the amendment of certain parts of Article 16. The 1921 League Assembly therefore proposed four amendments to Article 16, and out-lined 19 resolutions which should 'constitute guidance to the Council and members of the League in connection with the application of Article 16'. The suggested changes and guide-lines were an attempt to reconcile members' rights to decide for themselves whether or not a breach of the Covenant had occurred with the duty of the Council to draw up joint eco-nomic action once a breach had been established. They also counselled that the measures to be prescribed should be 'of increased stringency', starting with the breaking-off of diplo-matic relations. It was not possible to decide in advance and in detail what economic, commercial or financial measures could be taken in cases which might arise.[10]

Britain, and many other countries, accepted the amend-ments to Article 16. France, however, refused to follow suit, and so the amendments were left on the table, not formally adopted and yet furnishing a clear indication of the way in which many League members would interpret and carry out their obligations if the need arose. Indeed, as we shall see, in 1935 they were adopted as guiding directives when the League decided to apply economic sanctions against Italy. But in the early 1920s, the failure to adopt the amendments underlined once again the wide gulf which existed between British and French conceptions of how the League should operate; how it could most effectively secure international peace in the future, and resolve potentially dangerous con-flicts. Where the two major powers were willing to work together to resolve territorial disputes, the League could operate effectively to impose a solution, but when they were in disagreement, League mechanisms simply could not work.

Three European disputes, between 1921 and 1925, illus-trate this very clearly. In 1921, Yugoslavian troops occupied northern areas of Albania. Britain alerted the League to the situation under Article 11, and in his telegram to the Secretary-General, Lloyd George even hinted that economic sanctions might be necessary to force the Yugoslavian troops to withdraw. Ten days later, when the League Council met to deal with the crisis, the troops had been withdrawn, and the Yugoslav government agreed formally to respect the Albanian frontiers which had recently been defined by the Conference of Ambassadors. Again in 1925, when Greek troops invaded Bulgaria, the Council met quickly to deal with the dispute and the Italian representative suggested the imposition of economic sanctions against Greece. The British Cabinet also authorised Foreign Secretary Austen Chamberlain to agree to a joint naval demonstration off Piraeus if Greek troops were not withdrawn, and the French government endorsed a tough stance. The firm resolve and clearly-expressed intentions of the Council were sufficient to persuade the Greek government to withdraw its troops, and the dispute was settled without the need for the League to resort to force.[11] On both occasions, Britain and France worked together in an area of Europe whose instability had contributed so much to the outbreak of war in 1914 and where it was crucial that the League should be seen to be able to act firmly and decisively. The Yugoslav and Greek coastlines were vulnerable to naval pressure, and their populations to economic sanctions. Therefore threats could be made in the expectation that further action would follow if necessary. In neither case did it prove to be necessary.

The situation was markedly different in the late summer of 1923, when an Italian official working as part of an official delegation delimiting the Greek–Albanian frontier on behalf of the Conference of Ambassadors was murdered. It was a remote area, and there was no clear evidence to suggest whether the murderers were Greek or Albanian, or of a completely different nationality; nonetheless, Mussolini immediately addressed an ultimatum to the Greek government demanding apologies, a Greek enquiry into the circumstances of the crime in the presence of the Italian military attaché to be completed within five days, and the execution of all guilty parties. Furthermore, Greece was to pay a penalty of 50 million lire – about half a million pounds sterling – to Italy. While Greece agreed to many of the Italian demands, it refused Italian participation in an enquiry, and refused also to pay the financial penalty unless the enquiry revealed that a Greek was involved in the murder, in which case the Greek government was prepared to offer compensation to the families of those murdered. If Italy was not satisfied with this response, Greece would submit the dispute to the League and would accept its decisions.

The Italian response was to send troops to seize the Mediterranean island of Corfu, as a demonstration of Italy's resolve to exact due reparation from Greece. In response, the Greek government appealed to both the League and to the Conference of Ambassadors for help to regain Corfu and agreed to abide by any conditions either body might impose on Greece, provided Italian troops were forced to leave the island. The appeal to the two bodies gave Mussolini the opportunity to play off one against the other and to challenge the competence of the League to take action, on the grounds that the dispute had arisen out of issues solely within the jurisdiction of the Conference of Ambassadors. However, the League Assembly was about to convene in Geneva, and the mood was strong amongst the arriving delegates that the League needed to act firmly in the face of such blatant Italian aggression.

As Lord Robert Cecil, Britain's principal League delegate, wrote to Prime Minister Stanley Baldwin on 1 September: 'It is life and death for the League, and we must bring the Italians to reason even if it requires a League blockade to do so.' [12] Even Curzon, who had hitherto championed a consultative rather than coercive League, emphasised to Cecil his desire to 'support the League on the first occasion on which a small power has appealed to it against the high-handed action of a Great Power. I do not know what the attitude of the other members of the Council will be if faced with the defiance of the Council by one of its powerful members. But you may rely upon the support of His Majesty's Government in upholding the Covenant.' And to Baldwin, on holiday in Aix-les-Bains in France, Curzon telegraphed: 'Italy's conduct is violent and inexcusable. And if we do not back up the appeal to the League, that institution may as well shut its doors.' [13]

At Geneva, therefore, Cecil took the lead in urging the League Council to examine the dispute, and to take the necessary steps to settle it. But not only did he face the obstruction of the Italian representatives, who described the British delegation to Mussolini as 'hostile and cold', he also met with less overt but more insidious obstruction from the French delegates. They made it clear that the French government was not keen to engage in strong action against Italy, or even to admit that the League had competence in the Corfu Crisis.

Since the beginning of 1923, the French had been embroiled in an occupation of the Ruhr in an attempt to seize reparations due from Germany. This aggressive action had been condemned by the British, and voices had been raised suggesting that Britain should refer the crisis to the League for settlement. The Italians had stood firmly by the French, resisting calls to put reparations or treaty breaches onto

League agendas, and now they sought the assistance of the French government in keeping their Corfu occupation away from serious examination and action by the League Council.

By 4 September, Cecil was informing Curzon that the French representatives 'are unfortunately not behaving quite straightly' and that Poincaré, the French Prime Minister, was 'encouraging the Italians to resist'. There was a general French desire 'to find some way of saving the Italian face', and Cecil's suggestion to the French delegation of the possibility of a joint Anglo-French naval demonstration off the coast of Corfu to force Italian evacuation of the island was 'received coldly by the French'. Meanwhile, the Italians were threatening to withdraw from the League if the dispute was not handed over to the Conference of Ambassadors to settle.[14]

By the end of the first week of September, anti-Italian feeling at Geneva was growing very strong, especially amongst the representatives of smaller League powers. But in the face of tacit French collusion with Italy to challenge the competence of the League to deal with the crisis, what measures could be taken by the League Council? In London, the Treasury was very pessimistic about the impact of economic sanctions, with the United States out of the League and France clearly not prepared to support such measures. If they were invoked, the biggest loser might well be Britain, because of the damage to her own worldwide trade. Meanwhile, the Admiralty advised the British government that a blockade, to be effective, would necessitate a declaration of war on Italy, the concentration of the British fleet in Mediterranean waters to contain or destroy the Italian fleet, and the creation of large anti-submarine, minesweeping and other auxiliary forces to deal with Italian submarines and mine-laying. They concluded that 'in time, a close blockade of the

Italian coast could no doubt be achieved, but the magnitude of the operation should not be lost sight of …'. Meanwhile, the British Mediterranean fleet was 'holding a watching brief in the Near East' against Turkey, and was not in a position to take immediate and serious measures against the Italian navy.[15] In view of British economic and naval vulnerability in the Mediterranean and the continuing Italian intransigence towards the League, which had covert French support, the British government reluctantly decided to switch its approach from a League solution to an agreement brokered by the Conference of Ambassadors, as long as this included the Italian evacuation of Corfu.

Lord Cecil accordingly switched his efforts to ensure that the two bodies kept in close touch with each other and that the Conference of Ambassadors was sent up-to-date minutes of Council proceedings and proposals for settlement. The spotlight shifted to Paris, where after endless meetings and protracted negotiations, which the British delegate Lord Crewe described as 'exceedingly troublesome', the Conference of Ambassadors managed to secure agreement that the Italians would evacuate Corfu at the end of September, provided that the Greek government paid the Italians 50 million lire if the murderers of Tellini, the Italian official, were not apprehended. The crisis was over, but the manner of its conclusion raised serious issues about the authority and workings of the League.

While the British Prime Minister took a sanguine view, telling the Imperial Conference the next month that 'had the League not existed and acted as it did a resort to arms would almost inevitably have taken place', and his Chancellor of the Exchequer, Neville Chamberlain, suggested that 'if there had been no League, Corfu would never have been evacuated', others were more alarmed. Cecil's view was that 'the events of the last two weeks have ... gravely impaired the general confidence that the obligations of the Covenant will be legally accepted and carried out' and League Secretary-General Eric Drummond believed that the crisis had 'weakened the moral authority of the Council ... the authority of the League has been challenged in a sphere precisely that for which it was created and ... this challenge has brought into question the fundamental principles which lie at the root of the new world order established by the League'.[16]

The Corfu Crisis had clearly demonstrated that while the threat of sanctions might be effective against small powers in certain areas, it was unlikely to work effectively against Great Powers who were determined and militarily prepared. Furthermore, unless the other Great Powers, and especially Britain and France, were willing to work closely together to resolve disputes involving fellow Council members, and to take joint economic and, if necessary, naval or military action, the League could not exercise its authority in an effective way. This was a lesson not lost on Lord Cecil, who was well aware that the League could only be successful if Britain and France were prepared to work together at Geneva to resolve their differences.

As one of the major architects of the League, Cecil had been a commanding figure at League Assemblies since 1920, though, at General Smuts' invitation, as a representative of South Africa. Cecil had resigned from the British government in November 1918, largely as a result of his personal dislike of Lloyd George, and this gave him a wide degree of latitude to express his personal opinions and to operate freely at Geneva. Already in 1922, he was searching for ways to promote closer relations between Britain and France. His suggested method

87

was to tighten up the Covenant in some way, provided that the security generated would result in armament limitation, thus making the French feel less exposed and less nervous about the so-called 'gaps' in the Covenant and at the same time making the League a more authoritative international body. Cecil accepted that this approach might increase the possibility of coercive League action, but believed that the benefits – disarmament and a more amenable French government – would be worth the risks.

In the summer of 1922, Cecil was instrumental in drawing up a set of proposals linking security with disarmament, which he cast in the form of a treaty. Its most notable feature was that the signatory powers would pledge themselves to go to the assistance of any of their number who was attacked, providing that that country had carried out any armament limitation agreed by the signatory powers under the terms of the treaty. However, the obligation of assistance was only to apply to the continent in which the signatory power was situated, the treaty was to be an addition to the Covenant, and any non-members of the League could adhere to it. Cecil discussed his proposals with close friends in the British League of Nations Union and circulated them widely amongst fellow politicians, Geneva delegates and government officials.

The British Admiralty and War Office were scathing about whether signatories would in practice act in good faith and honour their commitments, and dismissed the regional limitation as unworkable. All they saw was a whole host of extra potential obligations and military or naval burdens, for no tangible gain. Foreign Office officials, though more sympathetic, suggested that Britain's approach to Cecil's proposal should be 'one of mild approval and benevolence, coupled with a determination to shelve any such proposals *sine die* [without fixing a day for future action]'.[17] Press comment was more favourable, finding Cecil's ideas interesting and worth following up, though *The Times* wondered whether the time was yet ripe for the discussion of such a scheme, in view of the 'suspicion and mistrust and territorial uncertainties that are the sequel to war'.[18]

After much discussion and some amendment at the 1922 League Assembly, Cecil's proposals were embodied in a Resolution passed by the Assembly and sent for comment to the governments of all League members. Half did not reply, including the British government, whose service departments predictably found the proposals in the Resolution premature and dangerous. Many governments agreed with Britain that the Resolution went too far, but others, such as the French government and its Eastern European allies, argued that a general treaty could not provide the security that they required and would need to be supplemented by special treaties which provided for immediate joint action according to prearranged plans worked out by the relevant military authorities working together. A member of the French military establishment, Colonel Edouard Réquin, tried to bridge the gap by linking a scheme of guarantees with disarmament, though not surprisingly, the emphasis in his proposals was firmly on the general and regional guarantees to be concluded. Only when exposed states were satisfied that help would be forthcoming in a crisis would they make suggestions as to what reduction of armaments they could accept.

In the summer of 1923, Cecil and Réquin worked together and helped to produce a single text which embodied the principle of a general treaty entered into by all contracting powers, who could, if they wanted, form defensive groups under certain fixed conditions. The scheme outlined in this text was referred to as the draft treaty of mutual assistance, and was considered at the 1923 League Assembly. By this time, Britain had a Conservative government which, since May, had been led by Stanley Baldwin, and Baldwin immediately appointed Lord Cecil to the Cabinet post of Lord Privy Seal with responsibility for League of Nations affairs. Cecil thus found himself at Geneva in September 1923 in an extremely difficult position, trying to seek Assembly approval for a draft treaty of mutual assistance to which his own government entertained the strongest possible objections. The Assembly, as we have already seen, was dominated by the Corfu Crisis, which inevitably raised a number of issues about League obligations and the extent to which states would meet them in future crises. Thus the draft treaty was not endorsed by the Assembly, but it was agreed that it should be submitted to all member governments for their scrutiny and opinions, as well as to non-League powers.

Opposition to the draft treaty came, not surprisingly, from the three major non-League members – the United States, Russia and Germany. France and Italy, however, were generally supportive, as were Poland, Czechoslovakia, Belgium, the Baltic states and Finland. But Britain's was the decisive voice – and by the time the treaty came to be considered in Britain, Baldwin's government had lost a general election, and a new minority Labour administration under Ramsay MacDonald had taken office. Those on the left of the Labour Party opposed the whole idea of promoting disarmament by guaranteeing security, arguing that security could only be achieved through disarmament. MacDonald had considerable sympathy with this viewpoint, and with a further argument of those across the party spectrum, that the draft treaty would stereotype the territorial settlement in Europe and would prevent any revision of the Treaty of Versailles. The Committee of Imperial Defence, which MacDonald authorised to examine the treaty, came up with a raft of objections to it, including the almost unlimited naval, military and air commitments which Britain would have to shoulder under the treaty and which would necessitate an increase, not a decrease, in armaments, and the likelihood that defensive agreements concluded under the draft scheme would degenerate into systems of alliances of the kind which had provoked the outbreak of the First World War. Britain's rejection of the treaty was echoed by the British Dominions, and though Latin American countries for the most part did not furnish a reply to the League, they in fact shared the views of the British Dominions that the treaty would increase their commitments and so reduce, rather than enhance, their security. The Scandinavian members and the Netherlands were also unhappy about the draft treaty, and despite the fact that 16 members accepted it in principle, including France, Italy and Japan, the treaty was effectively dead.

But the problem of French insecurity remained, and Mac-Donald was fully aware that he could not make progress in terms of pacifying Europe, and resolving the problems arising from the Ruhr occupation and the collapse of the German currency unless he could forge a close and constructive working relationship with the new French Prime Minister Edouard Herriot, a socialist who had recently replaced the hard-line Poincaré. MacDonald's first priorities were to resolve economic problems and to conclude a stable reparations agreement; but he promised Herriot that once these had been tackled, he was willing to try to find some way of addressing French fears about a future German attack. Both MacDonald and Herriot agreed to attend the 1924 League

Assembly and became the first leaders of their countries to appear at Geneva.

But what could MacDonald offer to Herriot, and what new approach could he put before the assembled League delegates? According to his diary: 'The newspapers had been announcing that I was to make a great pronouncement – and I had nothing prepared ... I talked the situation over with some friends, went home to my hotel, and put down a few points. Herriot suggested a consultation but I thought that would be a mistake. It was time for candid declarations and plain speaking.'[19]

Accordingly, in his address to delegates, MacDonald declared that military alliances would not bring about security, that the League must be enlarged to include Germany and Russia, and that the main problem facing League members was the problem of national security in relation to national armaments. The solution could only lie in arbitration – peace itself could only be secured by a proper system of arbitration. Meanwhile, Articles 10, 13, and 16 of the Covenant 'might well form themselves into a charter of peace if we would only apply them and fill them out'. A League policy should be developed to 'give security and reduce armaments'.[20] MacDonald's speech was very warmly received, though the *Sunday Times* of 7 September commented that his address consisted largely of 'platitudes, and the exposition of certain vague principles which met with very general acceptance'.

The next day, Herriot addressed the Assembly and agreed with MacDonald about the importance of arbitration. His suggestion was that a refusal to arbitrate could be regarded as a definition of aggression, and that an advance towards peace could be made by building on the three bases of arbitration, security and disarmament.

An Anglo-French Resolution of 6 September called for a disarmament conference to be held as soon as possible and the examination by the relevant Assembly committees of the questions of security and reduction of armaments, and of the provisions of the Covenant relating to the peaceful settlement of disputes and to arbitration procedures. With his obligation to Herriot discharged, and his words of wisdom delivered, MacDonald returned to London, leaving British and French delegates to work with their Geneva colleagues to turn soothing generalities into precise and workable commitments.

This was no easy task, given that at least one of the British delegates, Mrs Helena Swanwick, had been described as 'not only a Pacifist but an absolutist of the most unbending, uncompromising kind' and that the leader of the delegation, Lord Parmoor, had deep pacifist convictions. But a Protocol was drawn up which did include the possibility of military sanctions against covenant-breaking states, though Mrs Swanwick was consoled by the fact that the Protocol declared 'all war to be a crime ... it developed the system of arbitration ... aggression was defined ... and ... it required to be preceded by a successful Disarmament Conference'.[21] The intention of the Protocol was to make it impossible for any dispute which might arise to be left open. It was either to be dealt with by the Permanent Court of International Justice, if it were deemed to be a justiciable issue, or by the League Council. If Council members were divided over the merits of the case, arbitrators would be appointed to decide the issues and member states would have to abide by their recommendations. Thus the Protocol provided for compulsory arbitration, and if states did not submit their disputes, or refused to accept the final recommendations, they were to be deemed the aggressor and to be subject to economic and military measures by member states, in so far as their geographical position and condition of armaments enabled them to contribute. But before it came into force, a disarmament conference was to be convened at Geneva to agree a general programme of arms reductions and limitations.

The Protocol was agreed by the League Assembly at the beginning of October, and immediately signed by ten countries, including France and her East European allies. It was sent off to member state governments, and predictably received strong hostility and antagonism in Britain from the Service departments and from Foreign Office officials. But before it could be considered in detail, Britain was plunged into yet another general election, as the Labour Government faced defeat in the House of Commons over its policies towards Bolshevik Russia. During the course of the election campaign, the Geneva Protocol was widely used by Conservative candidates to damn their opponents and newspapers which supported the Conservatives ran a lively campaign against it. The most extreme was the *Daily Express* which told its readers two weeks before the election that 'Great Britain has ... parted under the Protocol with the control of her Fleet if a Socialist government is returned to power at the polls', and two days later, on 15 October, declared that 'every vote given for the Socialists is a vote for robbing Britain of her Fleet and handing it over to foreigners'.

The Conservatives won the election, and Stanley Baldwin was once again installed as Prime Minister. Back came Lord Cecil, this time as Chancellor of the Duchy of Lancaster, but again in charge of League of Nations issues. But he now faced a Foreign Secretary, Austen Chamberlain, who was determined to keep foreign affairs in his own hands, and a Cabinet which was strongly opposed to the Geneva Protocol and to what they saw as its unacceptable binding commitments imposing additional military burdens. Chamberlain was extremely sympathetic to French concerns about security and about future German aggression, but he soon came to the view that the Protocol would hinder, rather than help, his efforts to deal with these concerns. The United States was hostile to it, the British Dominions disliked it, and even the French government was asking for a bilateral treaty with Britain to operate within the aegis of the Protocol.

Once again, the British government rejected an attempt to strengthen the Covenant and to make its provisions operate in a more binding way. But again a British Foreign Secretary was left with the problem of how to deal with French insecurity which was blocking progress towards European pacification and towards disarmament. Chamberlain favoured an alliance with France, but many of his Cabinet colleagues were strongly against such a proposal. They were much more interested in a German proposal which had been received in January from Berlin that Germany should conclude security pacts with France and Belgium which would include provisions for the continuing demilitarisation of the Rhineland and arbitration treaties covering both eastern and western frontiers. They authorised Chamberlain to go to Geneva and, while rejecting the Protocol, give support to Germany's overture for a quadrilateral agreement of mutual security between Britain, France, Belgium and Germany, though only in very general terms. Accordingly, on 12 March, Chamberlain told the League Council that the British Government saw 'insuperable objections to signing and ratifying the Protocol' because of its provisions for compulsory arbitration and its addition of obligations to 'liabilities already incurred without taking stock of the extent to which the machinery of the Covenant has already been weakened by the non-membership of certain great states'. In Britain's view, the Protocol destroyed the balance of the Covenant and altered its spirit, suggesting that 'the vital business of the League is not so much to promote friendly co-operation and reasoned harmony ... as to preserve peace by organising war'. The more sensible way to promote feelings of security would be to make 'special arrangements in order to meet special needs ... by knitting together the nations most intimately concerned, and whose differences might lead to a renewal of strife, by means of treaties framed with the sole object of maintaining, as between themselves, an unbroken peace'.[22]

Chamberlain's speech was greeted with dismay by France and her East European allies, but with qualified approval on the part of the Scandinavian and Dutch governments. Back in Britain, the press was generally supportive of the new approach which Chamberlain had hinted at, but some Cabinet colleagues still needed a lot of persuasion that Britain should involve herself at all directly in guaranteeing west European frontiers. However, with strong support from the Prime Minister, Baldwin, and the head of the Foreign Office, Sir Eyre Crowe, Chamberlain was authorised by the Cabinet on 20 March to announce in the House of Commons that Britain would work with France, Germany and Belgium to conclude some arrangement 'providing for a mutual guarantee of security of the frontiers between Germany on the one hand and Belgium and France on the other'. Chamberlain had persuaded his Cabinet colleagues that 'if we refused to enter into any such arrangement and reverted to a policy of isolation, the only result would be an aggravation of the existing unrest on the continent of Europe, leading ultimately to a fresh war'.[23] Many months of long and detailed negotiations followed, but in October 1925, the Locarno Pact was concluded along the lines suggested by the Cabinet, with both Britain and Italy acting as guarantors.

Whereas the Geneva Protocol had epitomised the French desire for a strong, coercive League, Locarno revealed just how flexible the British government now desired the League to be. In some respects, Locarno had the appearance of a regional pact of the kind the French government had wished to promote within the framework of the Protocol. The frontiers of Western Europe were affirmed by France, Belgium and Germany, and guaranteed by Britain and Italy. There were provisions for security against aggression and for arbitration. However, no such guarantees were entered into in respect of Germany's eastern frontiers. Instead of resting snugly within a well-ordered framework, the Locarno settlement stood out as a supplement to an ambiguous Covenant, and furthermore, one that relied very heavily on the good faith of the parties involved. For since Britain guaranteed France against German attack, and at the same time Germany against a French attack, it was impossible for the War Office to make any concrete plans.

Furthermore, Britain was a party to arbitration treaties covering Germany's western frontiers but not her eastern ones – what did this imply about the extent of Britain's commitment to her League obligations in Eastern Europe? What would be the situation if a dispute flared up on Germany's eastern border with Poland or Czechoslovakia, and fighting broke out in Western Europe as a result? Would Britain intervene? Could she in practice limit her continental liabilities to Western Europe, and how did such attempts to 'cordon off' danger zones square with Britain's League obligations? Chamberlain's view was that the Locarno agreements strengthened the League, because they contained the important provision that Germany should join the League, and he envisaged that this would in the future enable British, French and German leaders to resolve their differences through direct discussions at Geneva, and possibly conclude further Locarno-type agreements covering eastern and south-eastern Europe.

It was indeed the case that for the next three years, with Germany in the League, Chamberlain, Briand and the new German leader Gustav Stresemann worked extremely closely together, both at Geneva and elsewhere, to resolve a range of problems and to give leadership to League members. But the underlying tensions and uncertainties persisted. At Locarno, Britain had given notice that it regarded aggression in western Europe in a very different light from potential conflict in Eastern Europe, and as the American historian Sally Marks observes: 'Locarno was widely interpreted as a green light for Germany in the east.'[24] The British Dominions were given the option of signing up to the Locarno agreements, but none of them did, which raised serious questions about British imperial defence commitments and the extent of the Dominions' support for military engagements in Europe. France had secured the British guarantee of her western frontiers which she had sought since 1919, but at the cost of weakening the territorial settlement in the east of Europe and of allowing Germany into the League, where she could press at Geneva for a general revision of the Versailles Treaty, and for member states to enter into the stringent arms limitation agreements to which they had committed themselves at Paris in 1919.

A recent historian of the League, Fred Northedge, concluded that Locarno was 'totally at variance with the League system and went far to destroy it'.[25] This is perhaps a rather harsh verdict. But what Locarno did was to reaffirm the diametrically opposed views Britain and France had of the main roles of the League, with France pressing for it to co-ordinate collective action and get member states to specify in advance how and in what ways they would counter aggression, and Britain wanting it to function as a flexible and consultative addition to more conventional diplomatic machinery. In the immediate aftermath of the Locarno settlement, these differences were pushed to the background. Once Germany had taken her place on the League Council in the autumn of 1926, the League seemed to acquire a new lease of life, and began in earnest to pursue disarmament and the possibility of concluding further limited security pacts. Even Russia and the United States were drawn in to the disarmament discussions, and this seemed to suggest the beginning of a new era of co-operation between the world's Great Powers, despite their ideological differences and the antagonism Russia and the United States had hitherto displayed towards League activities. In 1927, the United States agreed to a French proposal that she should sign an arbitration treaty modelled on Locarno, and the resulting Kellogg-Briand Pact, signed in 1928, appeared to bring the United States closer to Geneva. The signatories to the Pact agreed to renounce war as an instrument of national policy, and to settle disputes only through peaceful means. The fact that both the United States and Russia signed it appeared to confirm the growing optimism that enduring international peace, safeguarded by the League and by the Kellogg-Briand Pact, was finally being achieved.

But, like Locarno, the Kellogg-Briand Pact raised as many questions as it solved. It had no enforcement mechanism, and indeed, was harshly but accurately described by one

American senator as an 'international kiss'.[26] States might have renounced war in general terms, but Secretary of State Kellogg made it clear that 'every nation alone is competent to decide whether circumstances require recourse to war in self-defence',[27] a view shared by the British government. Thus states might resort to military action under the banner of self-defence which would be in conflict with their obligations under the League Covenant. Instead of bringing the United States closer to Geneva, the Pact emphasised the differences in approach between this growing global power and League members, and further exacerbated divisions between Britain and France. There were attempts at Geneva to reconcile the provisions of the Pact and of the Covenant, but little of substance materialised.

In the late 1920s, there was a palpable feeling amongst ordinary people across Europe that the League was becoming strong enough to prevent future conflicts. By the end of 1927, the French League Society had more than 120,000 members in 600 branches. By 1932, the British League of Nations Union had nearly a million subscribing members.[28] Both governments paid lip-service to the importance of their League obligations and repeatedly emphasised the priority they accorded to League membership, and to working with other great and smaller powers at Geneva. But in private, ministers and their officials were uncomfortably aware of the limitations of the League, and of how little it could actually achieve in terms of effective economic or military action against a major power, particularly in the absence of clear Franco-British agreement about how it should operate. As we shall see in the next chapter, its capacity to promote disarmament was also proving to be extremely limited. This gap between what people believed the League would be able to achieve, and what, in practice, it was actually able to deliver was alarmingly wide by the end of the 1920s. The onset of the Depression only served to further weaken the League's capacity for effective action and to engender widespread public disillusion towards it.

5

The League and Disarmament

One of the League's most important challenges – seen by many people in the aftermath of the First World War as being the defining test of League success or failure – was to bring about a reduction of the armaments of its members. There was a widespread perception in the 1920s that an arms build-up before 1914 had been one of the prime causes of the First World War, and that, in the words of Edward Grey, the man who had been British Foreign Secretary before 1914, 'great armaments lead inevitably to war … the enormous growth of armaments in Europe, the sense of insecurity and fear caused by them – it was these that made war inevitable'.[1] And once the war had started, new weapons technology such as rapid-firing guns, long-range heavy artillery, the first tanks, submersible vessels and aircraft had caused enormous physical damage and millions of deaths, not just of combatants but of civilians too. On top of this, the use of poison gas reinforced the fear of a new kind of warfare in the future – in which civilians could be targeted from the air or by mechanised ground forces, and in which navies could be attacked by new, powerful submarines. Thus there was strong popular pressure at the end of the war on national leaders to take action both to reduce levels of armaments and to place restrictions on the use of the more lethal new weapons.

The fourth of Woodrow Wilson's Fourteen Points had called for 'adequate guarantees given and taken that national armaments will be reduced to the lowest point consistent with domestic safety'. At Paris, the peacemakers agreed on stringent disarmament provisions to be applied to Germany, limiting her armed forces to 100,000, her navy to a small number of specified categories of ships, and forbidding the possession or use in future of submarines, naval or military aircraft, tanks or heavy artillery. The preamble to these disarmament provisions stated that Germany was to observe them 'in order to render possible the initiation of a general limitation of the armaments of all nations'. In response to German objections about various aspects of the Treaty of Versailles, the Allied and Associated Powers made it clear that 'their requirements in regard to German armaments were not made solely with the object of rendering it impossible for Germany to resume her policy of military aggression. They are also the first step towards that general reduction and limitation of armaments which they seek to bring about as one of the most fruitful preventives of war, and which it will be one of the first duties of the League of Nations to promote'.[2]

Article 8 of the League Covenant thus made it clear that the maintenance of peace 'requires the reduction of national armaments to the lowest point consistent with national safety and the enforcement by common action of international obligations' and obliged the League Council to formulate plans for reduction for member states to consider and act upon, taking account of the 'geographical situation and circumstances of each State'. Plans were to be reconsidered and revised at least every ten years and, once in place, limits of armaments which had been fixed were not to be exceeded without the concurrence of the Council. League members were also to interchange 'full and frank information as to the scale of their armaments, their military, naval and air programmes and the condition of such of their industries as are adaptable to warlike purposes', and the Council was to advise on ways in which the manufacture by private enterprise of munitions and war implements could be prevented in the future.

These were in outline very ambitious goals, which would inevitably prove to be almost impossible to achieve in the difficult economic and political climate of the 1920s. But the fact that they were contained in Article 8 of the Covenant, immediately after the clauses establishing the structures and procedures of the new body, testifies to the enormous significance which was attached to them. As Salvador de Madariaga, head of the League Secretariat's disarmament section, noted: 'Disarmament may therefore be considered as the first task entrusted to the League by the drafters of its charter.'[3] But the League Council could not impose limitations on its members, it could only make suggestions and take advice from a permanent commission of military experts from member states, which was to be established, under Article 9, to put forward recommendations in relation to arms limitation and to military, naval and air questions generally. And it soon became clear that military experts and government officials did not believe that arms limitation could easily be achieved, or that, if pursued, it would inevitably enhance national security and help to promote international peace. Cecil's scathing condemnation of the members of the permanent League Commission, that they did 'what their professional superiors at home desired, and that was almost invariably that they should do nothing themselves and if possible prevent anyone else from doing anything'[4] may have reflected his own frustration with the slow pace of progress after 1920, but it failed to acknowledge the genuine and intractable difficulties which inevitably hampered the pursuit of multilateral arms limitation agreements.

Sir Eyre Crowe, a senior official in the British Foreign Office, had made it clear to Lord Cecil already in 1916 that disarmament, though 'an attractive proposition' raised almost 'insuperable difficulties' in practice. Arms limitation could be carried out in different ways, he argued in a powerful memorandum, but each approach involved serious technical problems. Furthermore, not all the signatories to armaments conventions would observe them with the same scrupulous honesty, which would put deceitful nations at a considerable advantage. It would be difficult to find a fair basis on which to construct schemes, since 'the existing proportionate distribution of force is the outcome of history, of past wars and territorial arrangements ... At every given moment there are States who hope to retrieve past errors and misfortunes, and who strive to build upon stronger foundations the power of their nations ... To perpetuate indefinitely the conditions prevailing at a given time would mean not only that no State whose power has hitherto been weak relatively to others may hope to get stronger, but that a definite order or hierarchy must be recognised, in which each State is fated to occupy a fixed place.' If States were not willing to accept that outcome, then on what basis could standards of armed strength for various countries be worked out? Certainly, unless all the world's leading military and naval powers were involved in schemes of armament limitation, disarmament could prove very dangerous to those who undertook it.[5]

The international instability which followed the conclusion of the First World War, and the failure of the United States and of the new Bolshevik regime in Russia to endorse the peace settlement or to join the League of Nations, compounded the problems inherent in the pursuit of disarmament. France and her East European allies, convinced that Germany would challenge and try to overturn the provisions of the Versailles Treaty sooner rather than later, and fearful of the territorial ambitions of Bolshevik Russia, argued that their national security requirements necessitated the maintenance of large armies for the next few years at least. The British government, whilst willing to make drastic cuts in military expenditure, had a huge Empire after 1920 which necessitated a strong navy to protect imperial lines of communication and to deal with potential challenges from the world's second and third largest naval powers, the United States and Japan. In the absence of the United States, Russia and Germany from Geneva, it would be very difficult for the League to initiate any meaningful disarmament negotiations, even if the experts serving on its armaments bodies came up with approaches which might deal with the range of complex technical issues involved. For at the heart of disarmament lay considerations of national security and of political relations amongst the major powers, and unless these could be resolved, arms limitation agreements would be difficult to conclude. And yet the war-weary populations of the League's member states expected disarmament to be vigorously pursued as a principal means of securing international peace.

At the first League Assembly, a Disarmament Committee was established to advise the Assembly members on how to proceed. It cautioned that 'a comprehensive scheme of disarmament based on a thorough feeling of trust and security as between nation and nation, cannot be looked for at once'. There could be no real arms reductions before the ex-enemy states had disarmed, the League had established some control mechanisms to check that treaty agreements were being observed, and had also agreed a basis for collaboration with the Great Powers who were not League members. Meanwhile, member states should not exceed their existing levels of armaments and in due course a 'proportionate and simultaneous reduction' in armaments or military budgets would follow. Finally, members would agree to a 'comprehensive reduction of armaments under the supervision of the League to the lowest figure compatible with national security'.[6]

To assist the League's permanent commission of military experts with this programme of work, the first Assembly established a Temporary Mixed Commission on Armaments (TMC), which was to consist of independent civilian experts who might be politicians, economists, businessmen or labour leaders but who were to take a broad view of disarmament and to put forward ideas on how to advance its cause. Whilst the French and British governments were not happy with the establishment of the TMC, and Sir Eyre Crowe dismissed its members as 'absolutely irresponsible amateurs',[7] it was the individuals who were appointed to serve on this body who, in the next few years, came up with a range of different schemes designed to promote disarmament.

Two prominent British members were Lord Robert Cecil and a former Liberal MP Lord Esher, who was a close confidant of the British Royal Family and an expert on issues of British imperial defence. Esher agreed to serve on the TMC on condition that 'a vigorous attempt is to be made to come to grips with the two questions of disarmament on land, and the limitation of private armament production',[8] and it did not take him long to launch a purposeful initiative.

In February 1922 he submitted a series of propositions to the TMC, the main one being that, following the naval precedent set at the Washington Conference of 1921–2, the size of standing armies in peace time should be restricted by ratio on a numerical basis. Taking 30,000 men of all ranks as the unit (military and air forces only), he proposed that European states should have a fixed ratio of military strength, putting France at 6, Italy and Poland at 4, and Britain, Greece, Yugoslavia, Czechoslovakia, the Netherlands, Spain and Romania at 3.[9] He also proposed that the material of war should be limited by fixing budgetary appropriations for each state. How practicable Esher considered his proposals to be is not clear – he described them as 'drastic', and wrote to Cecil in August 1922 that they were put forward 'to show that a scheme of disarmament could be practically handled if the good will was there'.[10] But even as a starting-point for discussion his proposals aroused considerable opposition and resentment, and were attacked as being rash and premature by member states, like France, Belgium and Poland, who argued that until the threats to their national security had been effectively addressed, they were not in a position to endorse such an approach. Technical objections were also raised by the Permanent Advisory Commission (PAC: the body established under Article 9 of the Covenant to give advice to the Council and Assembly on military, naval and air issues) about the inadequacy of Esher's mathematical approach, which made no allowances for variations between one unit and another on grounds of quality of soldiers – whether conscript or long-service – equipment, or budget allocation.[11] Both the PAC and the TMC rejected Esher's plan, and agreed instead to pursue Lord Cecil's alternative approach of linking disarmament with the search for security, which, as we noted in the previous chapter, resulted in the Draft Treaty of Mutual Assistance and the Geneva Protocol.[12]

Meanwhile the TMC considered some of the other tasks which Article 8 of the Covenant had identified as being important for members to pursue – the regulation of the global arms traffic, the private manufacture of armaments and the exchange of 'full and frank information' by member states on their levels of armaments, military, naval, and air programmes, and the condition of their war industries. Here again, progress was painfully slow.

All the major powers had signed a Convention for the Control of the Trade in Arms and Ammunition at St. Germain-en-Laye in September 1919, and though this had not been organised under the auspices of the League, it seemed a promising first step to achieving global arms regulation. However, the United States refused to ratify the Convention because it would have greatly reduced American exports to South America as well as undercutting the domestic arms industry. The other major powers followed America's lead, and so the League drew up a new draft arms traffic convention, formally separate from the League, to secure American adherence.

This was considered at a conference held in Geneva in May and June of 1925, attended by 44 countries, including the United States, Germany and Turkey. Eighteen states, including the United States, Britain, France, Italy and Japan, signed the convention, but the conference discussions had revealed wide divisions between larger, arms-producing states and smaller states who were not able to produce their own arms and were concerned to ensure that their ability to buy arms from private manufacturers was not seriously restricted. Though Britain, France and 11 other states eventually ratified the convention, this was one short of the number required to bring it into force.[13]

There were close links between the global arms trade and the private manufacture of armaments, and the League Assembly was particularly keen to see the latter controlled at national, or preferably international, level, if it could not be totally prohibited. But again there were arguments between the arms-producing states which were reluctant to reveal confidential details about the arms production and defence preparations taking place in their countries, and the smaller, non-producing states who urged that full publicity was required to accompany any convention on the supervision of private manufacture of armaments to ensure equality. By the end of the 1920s, little progress had been made and the major powers stalled further discussion by arguing that further progress depended on a general disarmament agreement.[14]

Greater success attended the Assembly's efforts to outlaw chemical warfare, and particularly the use of gas, which had proved so devastating in the First World War. A special commission was set up in 1922 by the TMC to investigate the 'probable effects of chemical discoveries in future wars' and a report, which had taken on board the views of leading scientists from Europe and North America, warned League members in 1924 that 'all nations should realise to the full the terrible nature of the danger which threatens them'. Britain, France, Italy, Japan and the United States had already agreed at the Washington Naval Conference of 1921–2 that the use of poison gas was illegal and that they would not use it between themselves; and at the 1925 Geneva Conference on the traffic in arms, delegates decided to seek an absolute ban on its use. This was extended to cover bacteriological warfare, and the resulting Protocol for the Prohibition of the Use in War of Asphyxiating, Poisonous or Other Gases and of Bacteriological Methods of Warfare was unanimously adopted and signed by 30 states. Thirty-six states had ratified it by the end of 1932, though not the United States, who finally ratified it only in 1975! Nonetheless, the protocol was a great success. Although it was violated by Italy in Abyssinia during 1935–6, it was for the most part observed, and poison gas was not used during the Second World War or for many decades afterwards.[15]

Facilitating the 'full and frank' exchange of information between member states proposed under Article 8 proved to be much more difficult to achieve. While members were willing to supply the League with details of troop numbers, war material and national defence expenditure which were already in the public domain, they resisted any attempt to make them reveal sensitive information relating to mobilisation preparation or war plans, or to allow the Council to exercise any powers of supervision or of inspection over member states' armaments levels. More promising was a proposal that the League should collect and publish data on each country from official and public sources, and in 1923 the League's secretariat presented to the Assembly a report on national defence expenditure in 17 countries. Clearly an annual report along these lines could to some extent fulfil members' obligations to exchange information, albeit not fully or frankly, and the following year the secretariat produced an *Armaments Year-Book* which covered 37 countries. The Assembly approved of this as a 'genuine step' towards fulfilling members' responsibilities under Article 8, clause 6, and asked for publication to be on-going.

An *Armaments Year Book* was produced annually until 1938, covering over 60 countries, and accompanied by reports on the world traffic in arms contained in the League's annual *Statistical Year-Book of the Trade in Arms and Ammunition*. While Lord Cecil was scornful of all this endeavour, recalling in his memoirs that it never went beyond 'communicating to the League information that was already public property', nonetheless the resulting data collections became important and well-respected reference sources.[16]

By the mid-1920s, attempts to advance disarmament by linking it to the creation of clearly-defined security agreements such as the Draft Treaty of Mutual Assistance and the Geneva Protocol had failed. As negotiations between France and Germany for a Rhineland pact to be guaranteed by Britain and Italy moved to their final stages at the Locarno Conference, members of the League Assembly pressed for the establishment of a League body which would undertake preparatory work for a general Disarmament Conference. Despite the deep misgivings of the British Foreign Secretary Austen Chamberlain, who minuted that 'this is folly ... Busybodies want to do "something" and don't know what',[17] the Assembly agreed that the successor body to the Temporary Mixed Commission, the Co-ordination Commission, should consider the organisation, composition and agenda of a Preparatory Committee whose task would be to prepare a convention for a forthcoming Disarmament Conference.

In December 1925, the League Council formally established a Preparatory Commission, which was to consist of representatives of all Council members, and, by special invitation, those of the United States, Germany, Soviet Russia, Belgium, Finland, the Netherlands, Poland, Romania and Yugoslavia. Its task was to prepare a draft convention for consideration and adoption by a future general Disarmament Conference – deceptively simple in theory but phenomenally difficult in practice. For five long years, politicians, diplomats and expert advisors laboured to find some basis of general agreement while at the same time their governments sought to ensure that their own country's security, relative to that of their neighbours and rival states, was either enhanced or not in any way undermined. The arguments, interminable debates and frequent adjournments which punctuated the public sessions gave informed observers and peace campaigners a strong perception of deliberate obstruction and of selfish refusal of member states to live up to the lofty commitments they had undertaken as League members. But the reality – which we can see much more clearly now at a distance of some 75 years – was that the questions being considered were almost impossible for up to 20 diverse independent nations from across the globe to agree on through general multilateral negotiations.

The starting-point for the work of the Preparatory Commission was to debate and reach agreement on a number of general issues which the League Council had formulated. In F P Walters' words: 'How should armaments be defined? How could they be compared? Could offensive weapons be distinguished from those intended only for defence? What were the various forms which limitation or reduction might take? Could the total war strength of a country be limited, or only its peace establishments? Was it possible to exclude civil aviation from the calculation of air armaments? How could such factors as population, industrial resources, communications, geographical position, be reckoned in preparing an equitable scheme? Could there be regional schemes of reduction, or must reduction necessarily be planned on a world scale?' [18]

The Preparatory Commission, meeting for the first time in May 1926, added two further questions – one relating to the possibility of international supervision of the armaments of individual countries and the other to the manufacture of poison gas for use in war – and then established two sub-committees, one of military, naval and air experts, and the second of financial, economic and labour experts, to begin discussions. After six months, voluminous reports were produced covering armaments issues of men and material, financial resources, raw materials production and manufacturing power, but on all substantive points delegates had recorded disagreements, reservations or objections. So in a bid to focus the discussions, and to shift them from technical experts to political leaders and diplomats, the French and British governments each drew up a draft Convention, both of which were submitted to the League Council in March 1927.

What these now revealed were the strong and, in many areas, unbridgeable divisions between the two major League powers. In general terms, France believed that land, sea and air weapons and manpower had to be considered as a whole, whereas Britain was adamant that they had to be considered separately. With respect to naval reductions, Britain would only proceed on the basis of limitation by numbers and classes of ship as well as tonnage, whereas the French approach was to consider the limitation of total tonnage, irrespective of class of ship. On the issue of land disarmament, the French flatly refused to extend the limitation on those actually serving in its armies to include reservists, much to Lord Cecil's despair. The French, though, were happy to limit air and naval effectives while the British were not. Britain wanted the limitation of air *matériel* to be confined to first-line metropolitan units while France advocated a more comprehensive limitation covering overseas forces. The French wanted to limit land *matériel* indirectly, through budgetary limitation; the British basically opposed quantitative limitation and objected to budgetary limitation. The French demanded strict verification procedures while the British were opposed to any form of investigation or control by an international body.[19] Within a month, the Preparatory Commission adjourned for six months to try to find ways of resolving Anglo-French differences.

But this was no easy task. Each felt their own position to be absolutely justified by the political situation and by the nature of the threats facing them, whilst they found the demands of the other power unreasonable and unacceptable. The French premier, Herriot, protested that the 'Anglo-Saxons have ... this notion, false and dangerous ... that land armaments are perverse because they prepare for war whilst naval power has a moral value because it prevents war ... by opposing this viewpoint categorically we will avoid allowing the Anglo-Saxon powers ... dominating the world'.[20] Conversely, many members of the British government saw French ambitions to dominate Europe as the greatest threat to European stability, and were adamant that they would not offer France any security additional to the provisions of the Locarno Pact to induce her to disarm. Meanwhile, the German delegates demanded that the other powers should make progress in fulfilling their obligations under the Treaty of Versailles and left delegates in no doubt that a failure to conclude a disarmament agreement would result in a German demand to rearm, a demand which the British government at least believed would at some stage become irresistible. As Austen Chamberlain observed at the outset of the Preparatory Commission's labours, law or no law, treaty or no treaty, no power on earth could keep

Germany at her existing level of armaments indefinitely unless a measure of general disarmament was effected.[21]

The President of the United States, Calvin Coolidge, chose this inauspicious moment to sound out the British, French, Italian and Japanese delegates about the possibility of empowering their delegates at Geneva to attend a naval conference with the United States with the aim of extending to cruisers and to smaller ships the ratios for capital ships agreed at the Washington Conference (see Chapter 3). As de Madariaga observed, 'the calling of an international conference of five Powers to discuss one of the points which twenty other Powers were already debating with them was ... an unexpected action ... launched as if the League Disarmament Conference wasn't there at all.'[22] Italy and France declined to attend, on the grounds that land, sea and air disarmament were inseparable and should be discussed together, under the umbrella of the Preparatory Commission. The fact that the two powers were at the time engaged in intense naval competition in the Mediterranean was no doubt a more substantive reason for their refusal to participate. But the omens for a successful outcome were not good even for the world's three leading naval powers. There was no pre-conference planning or attempt to whittle down disagreements in prior negotiations. And the reason why agreement had not been reached at Washington to limit cruisers was because of the very different requirements of the British Admiralty and the United States naval department.

Put simply, Britain was willing to limit large cruisers but not smaller ones, and insisted that the need to defend the British Empire and in particular the sea lanes, which brought food and raw materials to her shores, necessitated a minimum number of 70 cruisers, the majority of them smaller cruisers.

The United States, on the other hand, demanded parity in cruisers with Britain, and wanted this parity to be expressed in terms of overall tonnage and not by category of cruiser. They envisaged a total of around 300,000 tons, whereas initial British proposals would have entailed more than double that amount, and their intention was to construct new large 10,000-ton cruisers, which would be able to outgun the smaller British cruisers and potentially pose a threat to Britain's naval security. As Winston Churchill, then Chancellor of the Exchequer, exclaimed, 'there can be no parity between a Power whose navy is its life and a Power whose navy is only for prestige'.[23]

Negotiations continued through the summer, with both Britain and the United States trying to use Japanese support as a means of forcing the other to make concessions. But it proved impossible to reconcile British and American objectives or strategies, and the conference had inevitably failed by the autumn, an outcome which was predictable from the start. The consequences were serious – in the first place, Anglo-American relations deteriorated rapidly, and remained bad for two years. As a result, Britain found herself virtually isolated on disarmament issues, at odds not just with France but now with the United States as well. And secondly, because of the obduracy of the British Admiralty and the refusal of the government to compromise on cruiser numbers or on gun sizes, Cecil resigned, removing from the Geneva disarmament talks Britain's most effective and influential representative.[24]

In early 1928, the Preparatory Commission was faced with a challenge from a completely different direction, when the Russian delegate, Maxim Litvinov, finally arrived at Geneva, his arrival having been delayed for two years by a diplomatic row between the Soviet Union and Switzerland. Litvinov wasted no time in criticising the assembled delegates for their lack of progress so far towards disarmament, and declared that only complete and immediate disarmament, involving the disbanding of all forces and the destruction of all arms, warships and war planes, would demonstrate their sincerity and produce results. After a two-month adjournment, the Commission reassembled and held a series of lively discussions on the Russian proposals, with many delegates attacking them as mere propaganda to undermine capitalist governments. But a serious point was also made by some speakers – that if the Soviet Union was really serious about working with other powers to achieve disarmament and international stability, she should join the League.

Once more the Preparatory Commission adjourned to see if some of the major problems dividing the leading powers could be resolved by direct negotiation. The result, in July 1928, was to throw the Commission into greater difficulties, when a deal was struck between the British and French governments whereby Britain would agree to the French demand that no limitation be applied to trained reserves while France would go some way to meeting the British insistence that naval limitation should proceed on the basis of class rather than of total tonnage. As news of the deal leaked out in the French press, indignation and anger mounted in the United States, in Italy and in Germany, and rumours spread of underhand dealings and of the conclusion of a secret naval agreement. The two governments were forced to withdraw the agreement and then cancel it.[25] Yet again, the prospect of some progress towards the conclusion of an agreed disarmament convention retreated from view.

With the election of a minority Labour government in

Britain in May 1929, hopes of a resumption of meaningful disarmament talks resurfaced. The new Prime Minister, Ramsay MacDonald, declared his intention to repair the breach with the United States and took upon himself responsibility for Anglo –American relations, whilst his Foreign Secretary, Arthur Henderson, with the able assistance of Lord Cecil who had accepted MacDonald's invitation to become a government representative to the League, started to formulate policies for positive action at Geneva.

The results were two-fold. A naval conference, held in London in early 1930, finally brought agreement over the limitation of cruisers and destroyers between the United States, Britain and Japan, when MacDonald proved willing to accept a total of 50 cruisers for Britain, despite Admiralty objections. And at the League Assembly the previous autumn Henderson announced that Britain would sign the Optional Clause of the League Covenant, which entailed the government accepting the compulsory arbitration of international legal disputes by the Permanent Court of International Justice, along with the Dominions of Australia, New Zealand, Canada, South Africa and India. But Henderson warned delegates at the 1930 League Assembly that 'unless naval disarmament can be made general, unless it can be completed by the reduction and limitation of land and air forces, the peace treaties will not have been executed, the Covenant will remain unfulfilled, and the peace of Europe and of the world will not be safe'.[26]

Two months later, in November 1930, the Preparatory Commission held its final session. The provisions of the London Naval Treaty were incorporated into the Draft Convention, and two further additions were to accept the principle of the limitation of annual budgets for countries' armed services and to propose the establishment of a Permanent Disarmament Commission which would supervise the execution of the convention when finally agreed, and deal with complaints about breaches. But the Draft Convention, so painfully hammered out over the previous five years, contained no actual figures, which were to be left to the Disarmament Conference to agree. And its failure to limit trained army reserves or non front-line aeroplanes, and the fact that it would not supersede the existing treaty obligations of states, such as Germany's armament limitations specified in Part V of the Treaty of Versailles, made it completely unacceptable to Germany. Russia declared the Draft Convention to be inadequate in every respect, and Italy and Japan also had strong reservations about it, though both the United States and Britain hoped that it could be improved at the forthcoming Conference once substantive figures were discussed and approved. In January, 1931, the League Council resolved that the Disarmament Conference should be convened for February, 1932, and four months later it invited Arthur Henderson to take the chair.

If the previous five years of protracted negotiation at Geneva had shown how difficult it was going to be to get 60 powers with very different national interests to agree to a single disarmament convention, the world economic crisis which unfolded after 1929, and its deadly political consequences, put paid to any chance of success. The Wall Street Crash of 1929 was followed by the rapid spread of a worldwide depression which drove nations to pursue unilateral economic policies to try to counter its effects. The political fall-out from the crisis was even more damaging, as spiralling unemployment and falling commodity prices and wages fuelled Nazism in Germany and ultra-nationalism in Japan.

In September 1930, over six million votes in the Reichstag elections transformed Adolf Hitler's Nazi Party from an insignificant extremist group into Germany's second largest party. A year later, Japanese troops stationed in Manchuria embarked on an aggressive campaign of expansion which was directed not just against China, but also against their own government which they believed to be insufficiently nationalist and patriotic. As the opening date for the Disarmament Conference drew close, the League Council was almost fully preoccupied with events in Manchuria, with plans to promote international collaboration to fight the economic crisis, and with fear about the possible consequences of a revival of German militarism. By the time the 60 delegations converged on Geneva in early 1932 to begin serious disarmament discussions, any realistic prospect of reaching meaningful agreement had disappeared.

While the delegates of the leading powers were well aware of the almost insurmountable problems facing them, their attendance at the Conference would, they hoped, underline to their electorates that they were doing everything possible to promote disarmament and prevent the outbreak of another war, and that if their efforts failed, it would not be their fault but that of another government. Furthermore, in a time of such crisis, the Conference would provide opportunities for safeguarding and for expanding upon national security objectives and for trying to secure the support of other nations for their aims. Events in Germany had intensified French demands for greater measures of international security to be agreed before France could embark on any further reduction of armaments, and for the continuation in force of the arms restrictions of the Treaty of Versailles. In Britain, the Labour government had fallen in the summer of 1931, and

MacDonald was now Prime Minister of a national coalition government facing severe economic problems. The declared policy of the new administration was that Britain had already disarmed to the absolute limit of national safety, especially in terms of naval power, and that her role at the Conference should be to put pressure on other powers, and particularly on France, to follow suit.

The United States shared the British view that France's military power, in combination with that of her East European allies, was the major challenge to the success of disarmament negotiations. At the same time, there were concerns about the sincerity of the Italian and Japanese delegates, and about the extent of their countries' military and naval ambitions.

But the greatest immediate political problem was the demand from the German delegates that if the other powers failed to conclude the substantive arms limitation agreements they had agreed at Paris in 1919, Germany would demand the right to rearm and to acquire weapons forbidden to her since 1919, such as tanks, warplanes and heavy artillery. For the German government, the Conference offered significant opportunities to win political capital which might help to keep the Nazis out of office. German rearmament had been taking place in secret since 1928, when the government had approved a five-year armaments programme. German delegates were well aware that the other powers would find it virtually impossible to reach agreement on levels of armament reduction. This gave them the opportunity to denounce such failure, and to demand that other powers agree to their right to build up their armaments and acquire a full range of weapons, thus legitimising the military expansion which the German army was pressing for and which was already under way. The French government possessed enough intelligence about what was happening in Germany to stiffen their resolve to refuse further disarmament. Other powers, however, especially Britain, were unsympathetic to the plight of the French, and warned that refusal to make concessions at the outset of the conference would inevitably play into the hands of German extremists such as Hitler. And as Nazi support continued to rise in Germany, with Hitler gaining more than a third of the votes cast both in the Presidential and the Reichstag elections of 1932, the political choices facing the delegates at Geneva became more and more painful.

In a bid to disguise the political difficulties, leading powers presented new proposals to the Conference, as if the Preparatory Commission labours had never taken place. The French delegate, André Tardieu, was the first to present a plan, on 5 February, which emphasised the need for new security measures to precede disarmament. Britain's new Foreign Secretary Sir John Simon made it clear that Britain was not prepared to take on any new international obligations and suggested that the Conference should start by trying to reduce or abolish 'offensive' weapons, though he was not sanguine that significant progress could be achieved, confessing before the start of the conference that 'I do not see any daylight at present on disarmament policy at all'.[27] While a technical commission was set up to try to distinguish 'offensive' from 'defensive' weapons, attempts were made by Simon and by the American secretary of state, Henry Stimson, to secure progress through talks in April with the German Chancellor, Heinrich Brüning, who put forward some fairly moderate schemes for German rearmament, including the doubling of the German army to 200,000 and the right for Germany to possess 'samples' of weapons forbidden by the Treaty of Versailles. But before any substantive agreements could be reached, he was dismissed from office by the German President, Paul von Hindenburg, and replaced by Franz von Papen.

The US President Herbert Hoover, facing an autumn election, now launched a sweeping initiative to cut the number of battleships by half, the number of cruisers and aircraft carriers by a quarter and of defence contingents by one third. Tanks, large mobile guns and most military aircraft were to be abolished and there was to be a ban on chemical warfare. While Hoover was only seeking approval of the principles of his plan, both the French and British delegations were furious at this attempt to seize the moral high ground, which was enthusiastically supported by peace campaigners, by the Soviet Union, and by the delegates of many smaller countries. While the two governments worked out the terms of a conference adjournment to give them time to consider how to respond to Hoover, the German government launched its own offensive: Germany would not return to the conference unless she was given satisfaction on the principle of equality.

The search for a formula which would satisfy both Germany and France now took centre stage and continued for the rest of the year. It was not until December, as a result of intensive discussions involving Britain, France, Italy and Germany, that the four powers agreed a short statement to the effect that 'one of the principles that should guide the Conference on Disarmament should be the grant to Germany, and to the other disarmed powers, of equality of rights in a system which would provide security for all nations'. Germany agreed to return to Geneva, but in both France and Britain there were statesmen who were under no illusions about the political prospect that was unfolding before their eyes. Herriot told the French military in October that: 'I am convinced that Germany wishes to rearm ... We are at a turning point in history. Until now Germany has practised a policy of submission, not of resignation certainly, but a negative policy; now she is beginning a positive policy. Tomorrow it will be a policy of territorial demands with a formidable means of intimidation: her army.' Winston Churchill told his fellow Members of Parliament in November that the Germans were not really after equality of status. 'They are looking for weapons, and when they have the weapons, believe me they will ask for the return of … lost territories.'[28] The accession to power of Adolf Hitler on 30 January 1933, underlined such concerns and set off frantic attempts by other powers to mitigate them. Mussolini took the lead in formulating a Four Power Pact which he hoped would bind Germany into an agreement with Britain, France and Italy to preserve the peace and work for treaty revision through the League of Nations while at the same time giving Italy opportunities to pursue treaty revision. It was signed in June 1933, but had no effect in restraining German ambitions. Meanwhile, at Geneva, the British had finally presented their own draft disarmament convention in March, which, had it come a year earlier, might have had some impact, but which now stood no chance of winning either French or German support, even though the new American President, Franklin D Roosevelt, recommended it to the representatives at the Conference.[29]

At the end of March, Japan walked out of the League in protest at the League's handling of the Manchurian crisis. It could only be a matter of time before Germany followed suit, and seven months later Hitler led the German delegates out of the Disarmament Conference and away from the League. Though the Disarmament Conference limped on for a few months, its work was to all intents and purposes finished. It had ended in total failure.

Many at the time blamed delegates for not trying hard enough, or nations for their hypocrisy in paying lip service to League ideals while in reality promoting their own selfish national interests. But in the circumstances of the early 1930s it was never going to be possible for national policy-makers to 'bridge the gap between internationalist ideals and the demands of national security'.[30] The political instability of the 1920s made disarmament extremely difficult, but the political climate of the early 1930s made the conclusion of a multilateral arms limitation agreement absolutely impossible. And catering for the varied armaments requirements of nearly all of the recognised countries of the world in a single convention was bound to defeat the ingenuity of even the most accomplished technical expert. Post Second World War international disarmament conferences would in due course be able to learn a lot from the world's first serious attempt at multilateral arms limitation, but at the time its failure only served to fuel growing disillusionment about the ability of the League to preserve international peace, a failure which was compounded by events in the Far East.

6
The Manchurian Crisis, 1931–3

On the evening of 18 September 1931, an explosion occurred on the Japanese-run South Manchurian Railway, just north of Mukden. The track was not greatly damaged – a train bound for Mukden passed safely over the spot shortly afterwards – but the incident resulted in the mobilisation of Japan's troops in Manchuria, skirmishes with Chinese troops around Mukden, and attacks on key points in the vicinity. Within days, Japanese army units had fanned out across South Manchuria and on 8 October, 11 Japanese planes attacked Chinchow, well down the track on the way to Beijing.

Three days after the explosion, on 21 September, the Chinese appealed both to the League under Article 11 and to the United States under the Kellogg-Briand Pact to take action to stop the fighting. While it was not immediately clear either in Geneva or in Washington whether the Japanese or the Chinese were to blame for the outbreak of violence, there was general agreement that the crisis needed to be speedily resolved.

On 30 September, the League Council accepted the reassurances of the Japanese delegate that Japan had no warlike intentions in Manchuria and no territorial designs and that her troops would soon be withdrawn back to the railway zone, and of the Chinese delegate that Japanese lives and property in Manchuria would be safeguarded, and adjourned consideration of the dispute for two weeks.

League members had far more weighty matters on their minds in September 1931 than military skirmishes between Japanese and Chinese troops in distant Manchuria. The British government had just come off the gold standard, and was in the process of forming a national government. Political events in Germany, with the explosive growth of both right-wing nationalism and communism, were profoundly worrying. European countries and the US government were locked in acrimonious discussions about the possibilities of reducing or postponing reparation and war debt payments. And energies at Geneva were being consumed by preparations for a disarmament conference and for talks to try to promote collective economic action to counteract the deadly impact of the depression.

But it was not just the timing of the crisis which muted reactions. There were a whole host of special circumstances which shaped the perceptions of League members as the series of military clashes unfolded and, within weeks, threatened to turn into full-scale Japanese occupation of Manchuria. The 11,000-strong Japanese Kwantung army was stationed in Manchuria quite legitimately to guard the track and railway zones of the South Manchurian railway, under treaty rights dating back to Japan's victory against Russia in the war of 1904–5 and to agreements reached with China in 1915 for the extension of the lease of the Liaodong Peninsula and nearly 700 miles of Chinese railway track. Since that time, Japan had invested heavily in her concession areas, and the

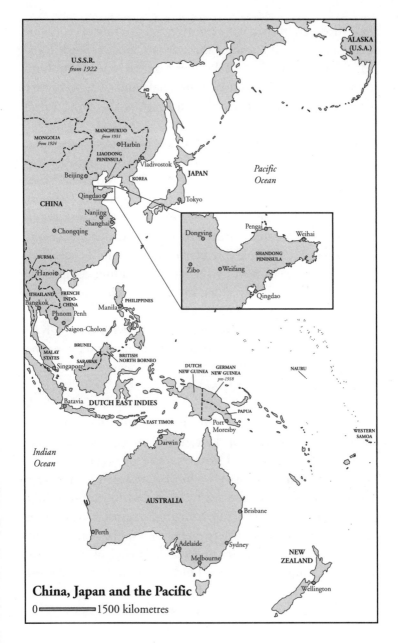

China, Japan and the Pacific

0 ▬▬▬▬ 1500 kilometres

industries established were contributing to a rate of economic development well ahead of the rest of China. Japan viewed Manchuria as an area vital to her future development, both as a source of food and raw materials and as a protective barrier against any encroachment southwards by the Soviet Union.

Japanese ambitions in the area were fuelled by the fact that Manchuria was not one of the 18 provinces of China, but was an outlying area, north of the Great Wall, and ruled, since 1911, by a series of independent warlords. Thus the Japanese portrayed their role there as one of establishing and maintaining order against unruly and corrupt Chinese elements and against the possible spread of communist influence. Such a stance was welcomed by the western trading companies, which operated mainly along the Chinese coastal areas, in Shanghai and around Hong Kong, and by their governments, who in the 1920s and 1930s were battling with Chiang Kai-shek's Chinese Guomindang government intent on wresting back trade concessions won by the European powers in the 19th century.

There was also a blatantly racial filter through which Western governments viewed Japanese ambitions in Manchuria. From the turn of the century, the right of Japanese immigrants to settle in California and in other American states had been progressively whittled away, while they were barred from Canada and Australia. As Balfour observed, it was therefore 'somewhat unreasonable to say that she was not to expand in a country where there was a yellow race', and as Field Marshal Sir William Birdwood, Master of Peterhouse College, Cambridge wrote to Lord Simon in 1931, 'she *must* ere long expand *somewhere* – for goodness sake let (or rather encourage) her to do so there instead of Australia's way.' [1]

Japan's strategic position in the north Pacific had also been progressively strengthened since the beginning of the century. As a result of its efforts on the side of the Allies, Japan had been granted League Mandates over the outlying Marshall, Mariana and Caroline Pacific islands, as well as having its rights in Manchuria acknowledged by Britain and by the United States. The Washington Naval Treaty had given it naval predominance in the waters of the north Pacific, and had pushed the naval bases of Britain from south China to Singapore and of the United States from the Philippines to Pearl Harbor near Hawaii. Neither power kept more than a small proportion of its naval strength off the coast of China, and both were painfully aware that in the weeks it would take for main battle fleets to arrive, Japan could inflict serious damage on British and American Far Eastern bases and interests. Thus attempts to limit Japanese naval strength were continued at the London Naval Conference in 1930, where it was agreed that Japan's cruiser strength should be 60 per cent of that of Britain and the United States. But again, given the worldwide responsibilities of the British navy, and the splitting of the American navy into an Atlantic and a Pacific fleet, Japan's superiority in western Pacific waters was strengthened.

Nonetheless, Japanese patriotic sentiments had been deeply upset by the outcome of the London treaty and by what appeared to be the subservience of the Japanese delegates to the wishes of the United States and Britain. On his return to Japan, one of the delegates was handed a ceremonial suicide knife as he stepped ashore.[2] And disquiet at the naval agreement was fuelled by a slump in American demand for Japanese silk exports and other products. In 1929–30, Japanese exports fell by some 30 – 40 per cent, and the price of rice and other agricultural crops also fell by around a third, causing great agricultural hardship. Because the army traditionally recruited from agricultural areas, feelings of despair, anger and betrayal towards the government were quickly transmitted to the lower ranks of the army.

By the middle of 1931, diplomatic representatives in Japan were reporting to their governments the emergence of deep-seated nationalist sentiment which was posing increasingly strong political challenges to the pro-western and pro-League policies being pursued by the government. And it did not take long after the Mukden incident for informed, locally-based Westerners to realise what was happening in Manchuria. The British Foreign Office received information by mid-October that what was taking place was 'a carefully worked plot and disguised scheme' on the part of the Kwantung army, which was preparing for further 'positive action', while Secretary of State Stimson was told by American diplomatic staff on the ground that the army was 'manipulating a separatist movement in Manchuria', was showing little regard for 'modern conventions of ordinary humanity' and, by 22 October, that troops were showing no sign of intending to withdraw from the main areas they had occupied.[3]

Such intelligence, however, compounded the problems facing the League Council, because it confirmed the existence of a power struggle taking place between the Japanese military authorities and the government. For the next two months, therefore, League members tried to handle the crisis in a way which would help the Japanese government to regain the upper hand, and this meant acting cautiously and refraining from any action which might inflame nationalist feeling in Japan.

On 24 October, the League Council invited Japan to

withdraw its troops in Manchuria back to the railway zones within three weeks, and suggested that this move should be followed by direct talks between Japan and China to settle all outstanding issues. But in Tokyo the Japanese government was already losing control over events in Manchuria. The army had invoked the 'right of supreme command' on behalf of the Emperor to take control of military operations, and senior officers in their turn were being pressurised by junior officers and by radical ultra-nationalists to support expansion of the army's area of occupation in Manchuria and to tolerate no interference by the League of Nations.

In mid-October, an extremist plot to overthrow the government and replace it with military rule was uncovered in Tokyo. Rather than punishing the perpetrators, senior army officers blamed government ministers for their weak-kneed and liberal policies which had inflamed the wrath of patriotic young Japanese soldiers and nationalists. Within three months, assassination lists of leading politicians and business leaders were being drawn up by a range of fanatical and extremist groups who wanted to express their anger at public figures who they believed had betrayed the interests of Japan or had enriched themselves at the expense of poor farmers and peasants. In early 1932, a former Minister of Finance and a director of the Mitsui corporation were murdered in broad daylight in Tokyo; soon after, Prime Minister Inukai Tsuyoshi was shot dead in his official residence.[4]

Thousands of miles away in Geneva, League officials and delegates were aware of the increasingly precarious position of the Japanese delegates who were representing their government at Council and Assembly meetings. Their concerns were shared by the United States government, who had agreed to work alongside the League to find a solution to the crisis, though it was made clear that US representatives could only operate under the Washington agreements of 1922 and the Kellogg-Briand Pact. Foreign Office officials in London learned in mid-October that the United States would 'back the League wholeheartedly' in its search for peace, but would disapprove of any action at Geneva, such as the despatching of a commission of enquiry, that would 'enable the military party [in Japan] to arouse national feeling and enlist national support' against Japanese Foreign Secretary Baron Shide-hara.[5] The British government was similarly aware of the strong sentiments being aroused in Japan. Sir John Pratt, an advisor in the Far Eastern department of the Foreign Office, warned the government that Japan believed that 'her exist-ence as a nation is at stake and ... will leave the League rather than submit to League intervention'.[6]

Caught between the rising nationalism engendered in Japan by the army's Manchurian expansion and the League's entreaties for a negotiated and orderly settlement of the crisis, Japan's Geneva representatives finally agreed to put forward a proposal for a League Commission of Enquiry on 21 Novem-ber, which was formally accepted by the League Council in early December. This satisfied the League's concern to apply the provisions of Article 15 to seek a peaceful solution, while the commander of the Kwantung army in Manchuria felt that it would be 'advantageous to make known the realities of the area to the League's investigators'. It would also give the army more precious time in which to tighten its grip over Manchuria and begin to erect there the 'façade of an independent state'.[7]

However, the army had no need to fear any immediate League reprisals. It was clear by the end of 1931 that the League's leading powers had no appetite for a confronta-tion with Japan and wanted to settle her dispute with China through diplomatic pressure and not by invoking economic or military sanctions. France, Italy and Germany were much more concerned with events in Europe, and agreeing to provide a member each for the League's Commission to the Far East was the limit of their active participation in the crisis. Britain had much more at stake both in terms of economic concessions in China and in terms of the protection of her Empire, but officials warned that 'a really hostile Japan might inflict serious injury on British interests in Shanghai' without needing to resort to military action, and thus economic sanctions against her were 'neither possible nor desirable'.[8]

At a Cabinet meeting on 11 November, the Foreign Secretary Sir John Simon reported that: 'As had been shown at the time of the Corfu incident ... it was not a practicable policy in a case of this kind to impose the sanctions provided for in Article XVI, which would involve the imposition of very drastic reductions on trade ... The only way to exercise any influence on the Japanese Government was to keep a representative of high standing at Tokyo. A third suggestion, that an international force ... should be sent to Manchuria, appeared inapplicable, since the Japanese were entitled to police the South Manchurian railway.' As Simon had briefed his Cabinet colleagues, Japan 'has a real grievance against China and the merits of the matter are complicated by a further consideration. This is not a case where the armed forces of one country have crossed the frontiers of another in circumstances where they had no right to be on the other's soil.' The crux of the matter was that 'every effort must be made to avoid the Chinese appeal being shifted from Article XI to Article XVI ... In a word, the policy ... should be one of conciliation, with the avoidance of implied threats' while at the same time upholding the authority of the League.[9]

The two major non-League powers also threatened by Japanese expansion had come to similar conclusions about the undesirability of a strong economic or military response. The Soviet Union was fully alive to the threat of Japanese northwards expansion in Manchuria, having, in March 1931, intercepted a Japanese telegram from the military attaché in Moscow to Tokyo which talked of an inevitable clash between the two countries 'sooner or later'. The newly-formed Special Red Banner Far Eastern Army was expanded, and plans made to send submarines to the Far East and to speed up the mechanisation of the Soviet army.[10] But half-way through a mammoth collectivisation and industrialisation programme, the Soviet Union was in no position to contemplate immediate action. A bad harvest in 1931 put great strains on the economy, since a high level of grain exports was needed to pay for the import of vital industrial goods. As a result, famine spread across Russia, striking particularly hard in the Soviet Far East, and the result was widespread discontent and disaffection. Stalin's sights were set on building up Russia's military power for the future; for now, the task was to watch Japanese action and try to contain it as far as possible by conciliatory means.

In the United States, the continuing decline of the economy was consuming public attention in 1931–2. Unemployment was rocketing in the big cities – 40 per cent of the Chicago workforce by October 1931, 800,000 in New York and over eight million in the United States as a whole, rising to nearly 13 million in 1933, about one in four of the workforce. Businesses were closing down, and over 2,000 banks failed in 1931.[11] Hardly surprisingly, President Hoover devoted most of his attention to domestic affairs, and left his Secretary of State Stimson to deal with the Manchurian crisis. But in mid-October 1931 he told his Cabinet that, despite Japan's 'immoral' behaviour, she had a good case for acting to protect her vital economic interests in a disordered China, and that 'neither our obligations to China, nor our own interests ... require us to go to war over these questions ... [Co-operation with the League over conciliation] is the limit. We will not go along on war or any of the sanctions, either economic or military, for those are the roads to war.'[12]

The United States Ambassador in London, General Charles Dawes, who was liasing with the League in Europe, conveyed this message to the League Council extremely bluntly in mid-November, '... the United States would not join in the consideration of the question of sanctions or in the enforcing of them if hereafter imposed by the League ...'.[13] The United States government did approve of the League's response thus far to Japan's aggression, and was prepared to allow an American to join the proposed Commission of Enquiry, but that was as far as Hoover and Stimson were prepared to go. The Kwantung army, therefore, had little to fear in the immediate future from the United States or from Soviet Russia, and indeed had every incentive to establish a strong Japanese position in Manchuria and in Inner Mongolia as speedily as possible.

Two further factors strengthened Japan's military position and sense of mission on the Chinese mainland. The first was the continuing instability and anarchy in large parts of China, and the failure of Chiang Kai-shek to co-ordinate a coherent response to Japanese expansion. He would neither agree to all-out negotiations with Japan nor to military action against her. In December, there were violent Chinese student demonstrations protesting at Guomindang passivity, but this only led Chiang Kai-shek to adopt policies of 'non-resistance, non-compromise and non-direct negotiations' which had the effect of weakening the position of moderate Japanese cabinet members, whilst reinforcing the perceptions of European and American statesmen that Japan's actions were, to some extent, being driven by Chinese lawlessness and petty obstruction.

Equally helpful for Japan's militants was the complete failure of Britain and the United States to work together or to co-ordinate their Far Eastern strategies. Indeed the crisis fuelled suspicion and hostility of each power towards the other. The intense rivalry over naval power, which had led to serious tension between Britain and the United States in the late 1920s, had not been dissipated by the London naval agreement of 1930. In 1931 and 1932, some American officers were writing of the need for protection against Britain. The Navy Board still viewed 'the British policy of domination of world markets' as being 'in serious competition with the United States. The British policy of naval supremacy is a potential danger to American territory and commerce.'[14] There remained in the United States strong animosity towards the League of Nations, and a concern that somehow European powers and especially Britain might inveigle America into action to safeguard European interests which would lead to commitment and to expense. On the British side, there was lingering resentment over America's attitude towards the recovery of war debts, over America's insistence on naval parity and handling of naval limitation issues. Distrust of America's intentions and policies was widespread in official circles. The Foreign Office's Permanent Undersecretary, Robert Vansittart, warned in January 1932 that 'the United States have often let us down' and that whatever idealistic sentiments they might express, 'there can be no active

American participation in European political problems in the near future. There will be no teething of the Kellogg Pact, or, indeed, any activity which by any stretch of the imagination could be described as the assumption of an obligation or a responsibility.' The British Ambassador, Sir Robert Lindsay, reported to London that the Americans were 'dreadful people to deal with [who] cannot make firm promises but jolly you along with fair prospects and when you are committed ... let you down.' As Baldwin commented cuttingly: 'You will get nothing out of Washington but words ... Big words, but only words.'[15] Thus if the cautious policies which Washington and London were pursuing towards Japan proved to be ineffective, the result would be that each power would blame the other, rather than working to try to co-ordinate some joint response.

Between the middle of December 1931 and the end of February 1932, the commission of enquiry which the League had agreed to despatch to the Far East was making its way to Tokyo, under the leadership of Lord Lytton, a former British governor of Bengal, whose belief in the League of Nations was reflected in his membership of the executive committee of the League of Nations Union. As the party travelled across the United States and on to the Far East, Japanese troops in Manchuria were advancing in all directions across the province, seizing Chinchow in the south in early January, and Harbin in the north in early February. Soon after the commission's arrival, a new, nominally independent state of 'Manchukuo' was established, with the heir to the Manchu dynasty, Pu-Yi, declared to be its ruler. But it was events elsewhere in China which now caused greater alarm to the Western Powers.

In February 1932, fighting broke out in Shanghai, the centre of Western economic and commercial interests in China.

Despite Japanese protestations that the Chinese had provoked the outbreak of violence, many commentators believed
that this was the beginning of a Japanese onslaught against
China. Fierce fighting between Chinese and Japanese troops
was followed by the Japanese bombing of Chinese districts,
which was vividly reported by the *North China Herald* and
copied in the *Manchester Guardian*. Readers were told that
'for terrifying ghastliness, the aerial bombardment of Chapei
is … appalling beyond appreciation … the Japanese aviators
came in lower and lower until at the time they bombed the
Railway Station they could have been little more than 300
feet up'.[16] The Japanese mobilised up to 50,000 troops to
drive Chinese forces out of Shanghai, all the time reassur-
ing Western Powers that they envisaged the engagement as a
limited one, and that their troops would be withdrawn once
it had been successfully concluded.

What response could the Western Powers muster? Both
Britain and the United States announced the despatch of
military and naval reinforcements to the International Settlement, but Stanley Baldwin made it clear to Parliament that
the aim of Britain was 'to bring about a peaceful settlement
… and to avoid embroiling ourselves with either side'. For
the United States, meanwhile, Stimson was sounding more
aggressive, affirming in early January his doctrine of 'non-
recognition', which he forcefully repeated in February when
he invited other Powers to subscribe to it. This boiled down in
essence to the United States not intending to recognise legally
'any situation, treaty or agreement which may be brought
about by means contrary to the covenants and obligations
of the Pact of Paris …'. Stimson also warned Japan in February that if the Nine-Power Treaty agreed at the Washington
Conference of 1922 was disregarded, the United States would

reconsider the military agreements reached at that time. To what extent his words would lead to any concrete action, however, was unclear, since Hoover had already made plain his reluctance to get involved in any war.[17]

The League Council, meeting a number of times in February, felt itself to be powerless to take any action which would halt hostilities, but a special Assembly, which had been summoned at China's request in early March, called for a cease-fire, for negotiations on the spot and for a withdrawal of Japanese forces from Shanghai. A week later, it endorsed Stimson's principle of non-recognition, reaffirmed the role of the League in resolving the Far Eastern crisis, and established a committee to monitor the situation and work to find a basis for its settlement. As far as Shanghai was concerned, the omens looked favourable. A cease-fire was agreed on 3 March, and facilitated by western diplomats, direct talks were held between Chinese and Japanese representatives, as Japanese troops gradually withdrew from the area. By May, negotiations had been successfully concluded and the foreign residents of Shanghai could breath again. But how influential League resolutions had been to this successful outcome was debatable; more likely was the fact that the Japanese army's ambitions on the Chinese mainland were very limited at this time, in contrast to its plans for the subjugation of Manchuria. Here, Japan's expansion had become, for ultra-nationalist groups such as the Great East Asian Propaganda Society, the base for Japan's struggle 'against the Anglo-Saxon world, as well as against Comintern aggression. In this holy struggle, all the peoples of east Asia must join to form the united front of the common fight with the oppressors.'[18]

The five-member Lytton Commission, assisted by a Chinese and a Japanese assessor, spent six months travelling around north China and Manchuria and visiting Japan, where they were left in no doubt by Prime Minister Yasuya Uchida that 'Japan would recognise the new regime in Manchuria, and that no outside interference would be tolerated'.[19] They summarised their findings in a report which was drawn up in Beijing at the end of August and agreed unanimously, despite the difficulties of trying to accommodate a range of views, including the French representative's insistence that Japan's actions should not be condemned. The report was commendably thorough, judicious in its findings and even handed in apportioning blame for the crisis in Manchuria between Chinese provocation and Japanese retaliation. It acknowledged legitimate grievances on both sides, and its only bold assertion was to doubt that the new state of Manchukuo had, as the Japanese claimed, been called into existence 'by a genuine and spontaneous independence movement'. Its conclusion was instead that it lacked general Chinese support and owed its existence solely to the presence of Japanese troops and the activities of Japanese officials.[20] Nonetheless, on 15 September, the Japanese government recognised the new entity of Manchukuo.

The League Council considered the Lytton Report at the end of November, and it was then debated thoroughly by the reconvened special Assembly which had first met in March. By this time, the Japanese delegates had made it clear that their government regarded the establishment of Manchukuo as non-negotiable, and that if Japan was formally censured for her actions in Manchuria, she would leave the League. Despite this threat, the delegates of smaller powers at Geneva, such as Spain, Switzerland and Czechoslovakia, were extremely critical both of Japan's aggressive policies and of the failure of the League's leading powers to condemn

them. In stark contrast, the French, Italian and British rep-
resentatives emphasised the complexities of the situation in
China, the corruption of the Chinese authorities and the need
for the League to conciliate rather than condemn Japan. Sir
John Simon's attempts to be even-handed in his criticisms of
Japan and China, and to try to get the United States and the
Soviet Union to work with the League to gain general acceptance of the Lytton proposals, drew particular scorn, both at
Geneva and amongst ardent League supporters in Britain,
after the Japanese delegate Yosuke Matsuoka was reported
to have commented that Simon had succeeded in saying in
his speech what he himself had been trying to get across for
ten days.[21]

While a League sub-committee was given the task of studying the Lytton Report and drawing up proposals for a settlement, Japanese troops were once more on the offensive,
this time in the area bordering on to Jehol Province. Every
advance the army made was rapturously received in Tokyo
by nationalist supporters, and the view that Japan should
resist any criticisms of her policy from the League, should
leave Geneva if necessary and face the consequences of economic sanctions or even war, was strongly supported by a
belligerent public. Clearly, the delay to establish 'the facts
of the situation', which League supporters of its machinery
for conciliation had argued so strongly in 1919 would allow
public opinion the opportunity to cool tempers and to urge
restraint, had had the opposite effect in this crisis. It had
instead given army leaders and ardent nationalists the time
to mobilise mass support for their expansionist ambitions.

On 24 February, the League Assembly met to receive the
recommendations of its sub-committee for an agreed settlement. They were largely based on the findings of the Lytton

Report and reiterated that Japan's actions had not been those 'of a country which has declared war on another country without previously exhausting the opportunities for conciliation provided in the Covenant ... neither is it a simple case of the violation of the frontier of one country by the armed forces of a neighbouring country ...'.[22] Nonetheless, it was clear that 'a large part of Chinese territory has been forcibly seized and occupied by Japanese troops and ... separated from and declared independent of the rest of China'. What was now proposed was a largely autonomous Manchuria but under Chinese sovereignty, a non-aggression treaty between China and Japan, and international help to participate in the internal reconstruction of China. Japanese rights in Manchuria were recognised, but the status of Manchukuo as an independent state was not. All the delegates present at the meeting, representing 43 countries, agreed to adopt the sub-committee's report except for the delegate of Siam, who abstained. The Japanese delegate was alone in his opposition, and after the vote he led the Japanese contingent out of the Assembly, having declared that Japan would still work with the League to preserve world peace. And while Japan did indeed participate in both the Disarmament Conference and the League's Economic Conference in 1933, her government gave notice on 27 March of her intention to leave the League.

There was one last act in the dispute. On 27 February, Simon announced that Britain would suspend the export of arms to both China and Japan, and appealed to other powers to follow suit. In fact, Britain was not a major arms exporter to the Far East, unlike the French, Germans, Czechoslovaks, Americans or Russians, and her embargo was likely to hurt China while having little impact on Japan. While Simon's initiative may well have served its purpose of satisfying his vocal critics in the League of Nations Union, whose protests at his excessively conciliatory stance at Geneva had grown very loud, it drew no response from other governments, and was abruptly ended on 13 March.

The League's failure to prevent Japan's occupation of Manchuria and the clear threat now posed by a nationalist Japan to Western interests in the Far East forced both the United States and Britain to reassess their naval and military capabilities in the region, and in Britain's case, led to the ending of the policy guideline laid down in 1919 that military, naval and air estimates should be based on the assumption that Britain would not be involved in a major war in the next ten years. Both powers recognised the urgent need to strengthen their Pacific naval bases, whilst British cabinets gloomily agreed that Japan would from now on pose a serious threat to the British Empire and to Far Eastern trade. But the crisis had also reinforced Britain's strong belief that the League only had the capacity to conciliate aggrieved powers and potential aggressors, and lacked the means to coerce them. The Cabinet was confirmed in its long-held view that the employment of economic or of military sanctions, in the absence of the United States, was totally impracticable and indeed dangerous, although another cherished British belief, in the efficacy of public opinion to cool inflamed tempers once a crisis had broken out, had been shown to be mistaken.

There could be no disguising the fact, however, that the Manchurian crisis and Japan's departure from the League had dealt it a serious blow, which was compounded within a year by the failure of the World Economic Conference and of the Disarmament Conference. Dissension with the United States over its attempts to mediate in the South American dispute and stop the fighting between Bolivia and Paraguay over the Chaco region – a vast area of undeveloped land – suggested that it lacked the capacity to operate across the globe and could really only function effectively in Europe.[23] The decision of the Soviet Union to join the League in 1934 helped to expand its geographical reach, but the factors which finally persuaded Stalin to send delegates to Geneva, the growing threats of expansionist nationalism emanating from Berlin and from Tokyo, posed a menacing challenge to the League's authority which required a strong and concerted response on the part of Britain, France, Italy and their new Soviet colleague. Unfortunately, Mussolini's attempt to profit from this situation, and the resulting Italian invasion of Abyssinia had, as we shall see in the next chapter, the opposite effect of completely destroying the League's credibility.

7
The Abyssinian Disaster

At the end of 1934, four major powers remained in the League, with the United States, Japan and Germany operating outside its remit. While Japan's future ambitions in Asia were causing some apprehension, particularly in London and Washington, it was Hitler's avowed intention to repudiate the terms of the Treaty of Versailles which caused immediate concern at Geneva. In the two years since coming to power, Hitler had revealed his ruthlessness by rounding on and imprisoning a number of avowed domestic enemies, such as communists, trade unionists and Jews, and, in the Night of the Long Knives in June 1934, even sanctioning the cold-blooded murder of some of his former supporters and party followers. A month later, Nazis in Vienna had assassinated the Austrian Chancellor, Engelbert Dollfuss, and sparked fears of a German take-over of Austria. Ambassadors in Berlin kept their governments informed of a relentless rearmament drive, and of non-stop propaganda delivered through rallies, radio and cinema, aimed at mobilising the German population and particularly its youth for future combat. On 9 March 1935, Hitler announced that Germany was building up an air force, and a week later the introduction of military conscription and the objective of establishing a peacetime army of some 550,000 men.

If Hitler's objective at this stage was to repudiate the disarmament provisions of the Treaty of Versailles, there was little doubt in the minds of Germany's neighbours that demands for territorial revision in Germany's favour would follow. In January 1935, the inhabitants of the Saar, having been governed by the League for 15 years, took part in a plebiscite, as provided for under the Treaty of Versailles, to decide on their future government. They voted overwhelmingly to return to Germany, in a display of strong nationalism which was fanned by Nazi campaigning. What would Hitler's next move be? To overthrow the League regime in Danzig? To remilitarise the Rhineland? To demand *Anschluss* with Austria, or protection over the sizeable German communities in Upper Silesia or in Czechoslovakia? Attempts at unilateral revision of the Treaty of Versailles in any of these ways seemed, by the spring of 1935, to be extremely likely in the near future.

France and her East European allies, Poland and Czechoslovakia, were the League powers who felt most threatened by events in Germany, but Stalin and Mussolini were also concerned about the possible scale of Hitler's territorial ambitions, and both leaders were willing to work with France and with Britain to try to keep them in check. The difficulty was that the Soviet Union and Italy had ambitions of their own, and as far as Mussolini was concerned, the present time seemed very opportune to pursue them. Mussolini had talked grandly for some time of his aim to turn the Mediterranean Sea into 'an Italian lake', though he knew that British and French naval strength there would be a major obstacle which it would take many years of Italian naval and air expansion to overcome. Easier gains seemed to lie in wait in North Africa, where it might be possible to link up the Italian protectorates of Eritrea and Somaliland to establish a more coherent and powerful north-east African empire. To that end, some action against Abyssinia, a League member since 1923, would be required, but Italy already had interests in the region which had been recognised by other powers, and particularly by Britain and France. Thus Mussolini made it clear to successive French leaders that he was willing to work with them and with other powers to contain German expansion, and in particular to keep the German army well away from the Brenner Pass linking Austria with Italy; but in return he would expect no interference in the pursuit of Italian ambitions in North Africa.

To the French government, consumed with fear at the revival of German military power and territorial ambitions, this seemed a price worth paying for Italian support. In the first week of January 1935, the French Foreign Secretary Pierre Laval travelled to Rome and held a number of discussions with Mussolini about the European situation and about colonial matters. It was agreed that France would make some minor territorial concessions to Italy on the fringes of Tunisia and on the Somali coast, and it was almost certainly the case that at some stage Laval assured Mussolini that France would not object to the establishment of an Italian protectorate over some or all of Abyssinian territory, provided it was done peacefully. The Italian minutes of the meeting suggest that Laval was imprecise and confused in what he said, and that Mussolini believed he had received a completely free hand.[1] At a conference in Stresa in north Italy in April, Britain joined France and Italy in declaring that the three powers would oppose the 'unilateral repudiation of treaties likely to endanger the peace of Europe', but the official talks did not stray beyond European issues, though it is very likely that unofficial discussions among some of the delegates did. The meeting was followed by the opening of formal military talks between France and Italy covering air pacts and the possibility of army and navy co-operation, and France also moved to conclude a treaty of mutual assistance with the Soviet Union, which was signed in May.

What Laval was not able to secure, however, was any firm promise of tangible British support against Nazi aggression, beyond the commitments of the League Covenant and of Locarno. Where France wished to organise military pacts aimed at encircling Germany, Britain was still hoping that conciliatory gestures might appease Hitler and draw him back into League membership and into rational discussions about armaments levels. Germany was not Britain's only concern; Japanese nationalist ambitions were clearly a major threat in the Far East, and Mussolini's ambitions might endanger Britain's naval communications and bases in the Mediterranean area, which was such a vital artery for the protection of the British Empire. Thus in June 1935, the British government acted to counter one of the threats it was facing by concluding a naval pact with Germany, under the terms of which German naval expansion was agreed up to a limit of 35 per cent of the strength of the British navy. For Britain, eliminating a naval race with Germany for the next few years would give her the time to deal with the threat from Japan and seemed to make good, pragmatic sense, but to France the agreement signalled British betrayal and an obvious breach in the anti-German 'front' which Laval was working so hard to try to construct. Once again the two leading Geneva powers were seriously divided, just as Mussolini began to put into effect his plans for Italian expansion in north-east Africa.

Italy had pursued colonial ambitions in this region since the late 19th century, but had the unenviable distinction of being the only European power to have suffered serious military defeat there, at the hands of Abyssinian warriors armed with modern French rifles at the Battle of Adowa in 1896. Since that time, the Italian government had sought agreements with Britain and France to adjust their respective colonial claims in North Africa and to establish an Italian sphere of economic interest covering the western part of Abyssinia. Abyssinia's application for League membership in 1923 had been contentious because of the prevalence of domestic slavery there and evidence of the active involvement of many of its inhabitants in the North African slave trade and in raiding neighbouring areas for booty and for slaves. Some members, including Britain and Australia, had wanted Abyssinia's admission to be delayed until these practices had been curbed but both France and Italy gave Abyssinia strong support, and she was admitted unanimously after her government pledged that it would do everything it could to abolish slavery and the slave trade.

Two years later, however, Britain and Italy came to an agreement to promote their respective interests in Abyssinia; Britain seeking to build a road from Sudan to Lake Tsana which entailed crossing 70 miles of Abyssinian territory, and Italy aiming to link up her colonies of Eritrea and Somaliland by a 1,000-mile railway crossing Abyssinia from north to south and to establish an economic sphere of influence in the west of the country. Abyssinia's government immediately protested to the League of Nations that such agreements were contrary to her status as an independent League member, and

Britain and Italy gave an assurance that they had no intention of bringing pressure to bear on Abyssinia, but that they
had merely wanted to regulate possible areas of competition
as between themselves. The agreement did not proceed any
further, but as Francis Walters observes: 'It was a striking
example of the way in which the pre-war diplomatic process
went on side by side with the new system established by the
Covenant.'[2] In 1928, Italy concluded a treaty 'of constant
peace and perpetual friendship' with Abyssinia, binding the
two signatories 'not to engage, under any pretext, in action
calculated to injure or prejudice the independence of the
other' and to submit all their disputes to conciliation or arbitration.[3] Despite this agreement, Italy was not the only power
at Geneva to entertain doubts about Abyssinia's claims to be
a civilised power with settled borders and therefore entitled
to League membership and protection.

In the early 1930s, Mussolini stepped up his campaign
to expand Italian influence in western Abyssinia, and an
increasing number of Italian troops were sent to Italian
Somaliland. In December, 1934, shots were exchanged
at Wal-Wal in a frontier area, and around 100 Abyssinian
solders and 30 natives serving with Italian forces were killed.
Italy refused to deal with the incident under the 1928 agreement, whereupon Abyssinia referred it to the League under
Article 11. For the next few months, various League bodies
endeavoured to adjudicate between the two powers, and
finally five arbitrators agreed, in early September, that the
Wal-Wal affair had been 'minor and accidental' and that 'no
international responsibility need be involved'.[4] But the inter-
vening nine months had given Mussolini the time to build up
his forces, and by the end of September 1935, large numbers
of Italian troops were massing on the frontier between Italian

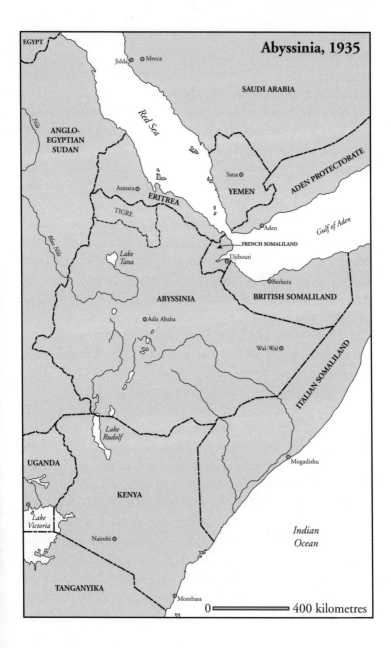

Abyssinia, 1935

EGYPT

SAUDI ARABIA

Jidda ⊙ Mecca

Red Sea

Nile

ANGLO-
EGYPTIAN
SUDAN

Asmara ⊙

ERITREA

Sana ⊙

YEMEN

ADEN PROTECTORATE

TIGRE

Blue Nile

Lake
Tana

Aden ⊙

Gulf of Aden

FRENCH SOMALILAND

Djibouti ⊙

Berbera ⊙

ABYSSINIA

⊙ Adis Ababa

BRITISH SOMALILAND

Wal-Wal ⊙

ITALIAN SOMALILAND

Lake
Rudolf

UGANDA

Mogadishu ⊙

KENYA

Lake
Victoria

Nairobi ⊙

Indian
Ocean

TANGANYIKA

Mombasa ⊙

0 ▬▬▬▬ 400 kilometres

Somaliland and Abyssinia, and a full-scale Italian invasion was clearly imminent.

If the French government was willing to accept Italian assurances that the military build-up was a precautionary measure to guard against possible Abyssinian aggression, the British government was not. In May, British Foreign Secretary Simon was warned by the Italian ambassador Dino Grandi that Mussolini was contemplating military action against Abyssinia and countered by saying that such action would have serious consequences for Anglo-Italian relations. The Cabinet was left in no doubt that Mussolini was poised for military action, that League action against Italy would break the Stresa front and drive Italy out of the League, and that all this would delight only Germany. Nonetheless, the Cabinet resolved to uphold its responsibilities as a League member, Simon recording in his diary at the end of May that: 'We have warned Italy in plain terms that if it comes to a choice between Italy and the League we shall support the League.'[5]

The Cabinet was no doubt heavily influenced in its decision by a strong wave of pro-League sentiment which was currently sweeping the country. In the wake of the League's failure to deal effectively with Japanese aggression in Manchuria or with disarmament, the British League of Nations Union had been mobilising its 3,000 or so branches to organise activities demonstrating the importance members and their friends attached to British membership of a strong and active League. A 'National Declaration on the League of Nations and Armaments' launched in 1934 had, by the summer of 1935, turned into a massive Peace Ballot, with half a million voluntary organisers distributing ballot papers to members of the public seeking their views on whether they supported the League and whether they favoured collective security and the employment of economic or military sanctions against aggression. The original aim of four to five million responses was greatly exceeded; 11.5 million people – about half of the number who voted in the two previous general elections of 1929 and 1931 – responded. League support was overwhelming, with ten million voting in favour of economic sanctions, and only 635,000 against, and 6.7 million voting for military sanctions, with 2.3 million against.[6] With a general election in the offing, there was no way that the government could ignore such strong pro-League sentiment.

At the same time, there were still hopes that some means might be found of adjusting Italian ambitions with Abyssinian sovereignty, or, failing an agreed settlement, that League sanctions against Italy might in their early stages be mild enough not to antagonise Italy but yet exert sufficient pressure to force her to the negotiating table. Thus the British government sought to deal with the growing Abyssinian crisis through 'a judicious mixture of new League methods and "old diplomacy"...', the means by which Simon had already tried, and failed, to deal with Japan over Manchuria.[7] It was not to be an easy or very effective approach, entailing as it did some serious ambiguities. Britain would take an active stance at Geneva in support of collective action against Italy to satisfy public demand, while at the same time participating in discussions with France and Italy to find a peaceful outcome acceptable to Mussolini, thus keeping him involved in efforts to contain German expansion. And a strong pro-League policy would be combined with frequent assurances to Italy that any League sanctions were aimed at impeding Italian aggression but not at completely crippling her. On 11 September, at the League Assembly, Sir Samuel Hoare, who had replaced Sir John Simon as Foreign Secretary, made a powerful speech emphasising Britain's support for the 'collective maintenance of the Covenant in its entirety, and particularly for steady and collective resistance to all unprovoked aggression' but also stressing that League burdens 'must be borne collectively. If risks for peace are to be run, they must be run by all.' Nonetheless, Hoare also went out of his way to acknowledge that 'backward nations are ... entitled to expect that assistance will be afforded to them by more advanced peoples in the development of their resources and the building up of their national life'.[8]

Hoare's concern to show not just the British public but Germany too that the League was serious about countering aggression was not shared by Laval. The French view was that the prospect of strong League action against Italy would merely drive Mussolini into Hitler's arms. Laval told Hoare that 'there ought to be no provocative talk of sanctions and no wounding of Italian feelings' and that if any economic pressure was applied by the League, it should be fairly mild and not have the effect of presenting a knife to Mussolini's throat.[9] Hoare told the British Cabinet in early October that Laval would only agree to mild economic sanctions, to be applied in two stages – a refusal to sell war material and perhaps key minerals to Italy, followed by a refusal to buy Italian goods – and that there was no way the French Foreign Secretary would support really severe sanctions involving a blockade or military sanctions.

The concern for the British government was whether mild economic sanctions would have enough impact to slow down Italy's campaign against Abyssinia and show that the League was able to take effective action. Hoare at this stage was willing to go along with Laval's suggested approach, and at the same time he told his Cabinet colleagues that he was still hopeful that a settlement could be reached in direct discussions with Italy and France which 'would not destroy Abyssinian independence but would give Italy some satisfaction'.[10]

Meanwhile, Britain moved its Home Fleet into the Mediterranean as a precautionary warning to Italy to refrain from any aggression against British bases or ships there, and sought an assurance from France that support would be forthcoming if a naval clash between Italy and Britain occurred. Laval made it clear that French assistance would be conditional on a prior British agreement to assist France militarily in resisting any attempt by Hitler to remilitarise the Rhineland. No agreement was reached and once again the two powers were openly at odds, each distrusting the other and neither prepared to take a strong lead against either Italy or Germany in case they were left to face Italian or German retaliation on their own.

On 3 October, Italy finally unleashed its invasion of Abyssinia, which quickly turned into a full-scale military operation, involving 400,000 troops by December 1935 and a further 250,000 early in the new year, along with air power which subjected Abyssinian combatants and civilians to mustard gas attacks. Within Italy, national support was whipped up for this military revenge for the defeat at Adowa in 1896, and a quarter of a million married women, including the Queen, donated their wedding rings to boost the country's gold reserves.[11] Four days later, all the members of the League Council with the exception of the Italian delegate agreed that Italy had resorted to war against another League member in flagrant disregard of her obligations under Article 12 of the Covenant, and that sanctions now had to be imposed, the first and only time in the League's history that Article 16 was invoked in a dispute. A plenary meeting of the League Assembly on 9 October endorsed this course of action, and a Co-ordination Committee was established to liase with individual members, whose responsibility it was to take the sanctions 'directly and individually' and to draw up an agreed list of measures. Only a handful of states, which included those who were most dependent on trade with Italy such as Austria, Hungary and Albania, and Switzerland who was concerned that taking sanctions would undermine her neutrality, indicated that they would not feel able to participate.

The Co-ordination Committee followed the guidelines which had been drawn up for the application of Article 16 in 1921 and which had suggested graduated economic sanctions increasing in severity if the offending state remained recalcitrant (see Chapter 4). The first proposals therefore were for four measures: an embargo on the export of arms and ammunition to Italy, the withholding of loans and credits, prohibition of imported goods from Italy and a ban on the export of certain key products to her. By 31 October, 50 governments had agreed to the first proposal, 49 to the second and 48 to the third and fourth. It was decided that the starting date for the application of sanctions should be 18 November.[12]

The Co-ordination Committee also notified non-members of the League of the measures which League members proposed to take against Italy and asked for their support. No response was forthcoming from Germany, Japan or Brazil, but the United States did signify its support for the League's efforts, though President Roosevelt made clear that he was bound by American neutrality legislation which had just come into force in 1935.

On 2 November, the Canadian delegate proposed

extending the list of proposed League sanctions to include petroleum, coal, iron, cast iron and steel, and this suggestion was forwarded to League members for their views. This would undoubtedly be a step too far for the French, but it also caused great concern to the British government, since Mussolini had made it clear that any such extension of sanctions to include oil would be regarded as an act of war. Once again the British government sought assurances from France of support in the event of Mussolini attacking British ships or bases in the Mediterranean in response to an oil embargo; once again the French response was evasive, and Laval made it clear that the French government would not support oil sanctions or any measures which involved the closure of the Suez Canal.

Growing Anglo-French friction, and the steady advance of Italian troops into Abyssinia, impressed upon Hoare the urgency of stepping up attempts to try to find some end to the crisis through direct negotiations with France and Italy. A number of possible solutions had already been discussed, such as agreeing to an Italian protectorate or sphere of economic influence over part or all of Abyssinia, or frontier adjustments in Italy's favour in return for giving Abyssinia access to the sea through British or Italian Somaliland. Thus far, no proposal had been agreeable to both sides, but by 18 November Hoare was telling the Co-ordination Committee that though Britain, as a loyal League member, felt duty-bound to 'carry out our obligations and to undertake the duty imposed upon us by the Covenant', at the same time 'we are under a no less insistent obligation to strive for a speedy and honourable settlement of the controversy' and that in recent days conversations had been taking place between Britain, France and Italy to try to find some basis for a settlement.

Though Abyssinia was not involved in the talks, Hoare assured the League that there was no intention on the part of the three European countries to 'make and conclude an agreement behind the backs of the League'. The Co-ordination Committee expressed its support for these endeavours, which, the Belgian Prime Minister urged, should continue under the League's auspices and control and 'in the spirit of the Covenant'.[13] But was it possible at this late stage to find an outcome which would prove acceptable to both Italy and Abyssinia? Italy sought a Mandate over Abyssinia at the very least, a proposal Britain was strongly opposed to, and so the bargaining continued. But in one respect at least the pressure lifted on Hoare, when on 14 November, the National Government, led by Stanley Baldwin, gained a decisive election victory over the Liberal and Labour opposition.

Difficult negotiations continued between Britain and France. By the end of November, the British government had agreed to support a package of proposals which included a League plan of assistance for Abyssinia, some territorial adjustments which would give Abyssinia a corridor of land leading to the Gulf of Aden, and the creation for Italy of 'a special sphere for Italian economic development and colonisation' under League supervision. Italy, however, wanted more, and Laval was intent on pushing Hoare into further pro-Italian concessions. Fatefully, on his way to a holiday in Switzerland in the first week of December, Hoare stopped off in Paris for more talks with Laval. Over two days of intense bargaining, he was persuaded to agree, subject to the Cabinet's approval, to a three-part plan which comprised a corridor of land linking Abyssinia to the sea at Zeila; the assignation to Italy, in exchange, of part of Tigré and territory in the east and south-east of Abyssinia; and a large area of land in the south and south-west of Abyssinia to be recognised as an Italian economic development zone under League of Nations supervision, though still under Abyssinian sovereignty. The net effect of these proposals would be to deprive Abyssinia, directly or indirectly, of just over half of its territory. The two men agreed that they should sound out Mussolini first about the plan and then inform Abyssinia's ruler, Haile Selassie, and Laval made his view brutally clear that if Haile Selassie rejected the plan, the oil sanction proposal would have to be dropped.[14]

As Hoare resumed his journey to Switzerland, the British Cabinet was hastily summoned to consider the proposals. Sir John Simon recorded in his diary that they 'seemed very much like "rewarding the aggressor", but the Cabinet felt that it was hardly possible to throw over the Foreign Secretary in his absence. So we contented ourselves with insisting … that the terms must be submitted with equal fullness to both sides – it seemed impossible that Abyssinia would accept them – and with refusing to agree … that oil sanctions were impossible if Abyssinia rejected the terms.'[15] But at this point, the 'Hoare-Laval plan', as it came to be known, was leaked virtually in full in the French press, and was picked up and strongly criticised by British newspapers. Simon's diary records the change in the mood of the Cabinet: '… The full gravity of the proposal became more evident. We learned for the first time that it was not intended to allow Abyssinia to construct an independent railway to the port and *The Times* attacked the scheme in a leader headed "A Corridor for Camels"…' The Cabinet began to turn against the plan, no doubt influenced by the rising clamour of outrage from League-supporting members of the public, and the Government's representative at Geneva, Anthony Eden, was authorised to tell the League

Council that the British government would not recommend acceptance of it if it did not have the approval of all the parties concerned.[16] But this did not quell the outbursts of anger in Britain at Hoare's 'betrayal' of the League and of Abyssinia – the Cabinet was informed that opinion in the City of London regarded it as 'the most miserable document that has ever disgraced the signature of a British statesman', and the Opposition was moving to propose a vote of censure on 19 December denouncing the Hoare-Laval plan as an attempt to 'reward the declared aggressor at the expense of the victim, destroy collective security and conflict with the expressed will of the country and of the Covenant of the League of Nations'. Sir John Simon warned Baldwin that 'this was very nearly what the Cabinet felt'.[17]

Hoare was by this time receiving hospital treatment in Switzerland, having broken his nose ice-skating, so he was in no position to try to stem the flood of criticism against his proposals. Instead, the combined weight of public and of political outrage resulted in his resignation, and replacement as Foreign Secretary by Anthony Eden.[18] The plan was withdrawn, Italy continued its military offensive against Abyssinia, and the League pressed on with economic sanctions. But the speed of the Italian advance made it clear that only more direct sanctions – such as cutting off oil supplies or closing the Suez canal – would have any impact in preventing an Italian victory, and such measures ran a high risk of inviting Italian reprisals or some 'mad dog act' on the part of Mussolini, which the British feared would inevitably be aimed at their Mediterranean fleet or bases. The Admiralty feared that a hostile Italy would pose a real threat to imperial communications and defence, when in fact the serious naval threats were likely to come from Germany and Japan. Rather than alienating Italy, the government should be seeking to placate her; as the First Sea Lord Admiral Lord Chatfield protested, 'this miserable business of collective security has run away with all our traditional interests and policies'.[19]

While Eden was nonetheless prepared to press forward with the imposition of oil sanctions, and the Cabinet agreed to support this proposal at the end of February, the French continued to object strongly, and to make it clear that they would not help the British to counter any Italian reprisals unless the British agreed to stand by France's side in the event of German remilitarisation of the Rhineland. But since the British Government was at this time intent on trying to tempt Hitler into discussions which would trade German remilitarisation of the Rhineland for an air pact and a German return to the League, no agreement between France and Britain could be struck. Oil sanctions continued to be threatened, but not agreed; Italian troops continued their relentless advance, unchecked by the modest economic sanctions being imposed; and the League continued to exhort Italy and Abyssinia to seek a negotiated settlement. Then suddenly, in the first week of March 1936, the situation dramatically changed when Hitler decided to risk unilateral action and to march German troops into the Rhineland, citing France's ratification of the 1935 Franco-Soviet Pact as a justification. This was a breach both of the Treaty of Versailles and of the Locarno Pact, guaranteed by Britain and Italy. The French government, facing an election within two months, turned to Britain for support. The British War Office, however, had already made it clear to their French counterparts that in the event of hostilities breaking out in respect of Rhineland remilitarisation, they could only offer to despatch to the area two regular divisions, which would take three months to mobilise. And the preference of the Cabinet was for negotiations with Hitler, since Baldwin and Chancellor of the Exchequer Neville Chamberlain believed that 'neither France nor England was really in a position to take effective military action'.[20]

Intense efforts to resolve the Rhineland issue now took centre stage. While the British government was willing to believe German assurances that if the Rhineland remilitarisation was not contested by Britain and France, Hitler would return to the League, negotiate a replacement agreement for Locarno, sign non-aggression pacts with all the states on Germany's eastern frontier and seriously consider an air pact, there could be no doubting the threat posed by growing German strength. The British hoped to contain it by conciliation and by negotiation; the French did not believe this was a realistic prospect, but dared not risk taking action alone. Both powers, however, agreed, that in this new situation, every effort should be made to obtain Mussolini's support, and that meant not taking any action at Geneva which would alienate him further. This stance was supported by the British Service Chiefs, who on 1 April reported: 'If we seriously consider the possibility of war with Germany it is essential that the Services be relieved of their Mediterranean responsibilities. Otherwise our position is utterly unsafe.'[21]

Italy continued its military onslaught in Abyssinia, seemingly unhampered by the fairly mild economic sanctions being applied. In early May, Italian troops entered the capital, Addis Ababa, and Haile Selassie fled. It was clear that the League's efforts to prevent the Italian occupation and defeat of Abyssinia had failed. While the French had at best been lukewarm in their application of Article 16 against Italy, the British at Geneva had taken a strong line. But on 6 May,

Eden admitted in the House of Commons that sanctions had failed, and a month later his colleague and Chancellor of the Exchequer, Neville Chamberlain, was calling for them to be scrapped, describing their continuation as the 'midsummer of madness'. On 17 June, Eden argued for their abandonment at a Cabinet meeting and, on receiving agreement from his colleagues, proposed to Parliament the next day that sanctions should be lifted. In early July, the League agreed that sanctions should be ended on 15 July. Abyssinia was absorbed into Italy's Empire, and Italy announced that she would leave the League; she left the following year.[22] With the outbreak of the Spanish civil war in the summer of 1936, Mussolini soon found himself working more and more closely with Hitler to help the Spanish military leader, General Franco, defeat his Republican opponents. And the League was further weakened, with only France, Britain and Soviet Russia left at Geneva to try to counteract growing and concerted aggression from Germany, Italy and Japan, with the United States standing resolutely aside.

Divisions between Britain and France had already undermined the effectiveness of the League in the 1920s, during the Corfu dispute and over the discussions around the formulation of the Geneva Protocol (see Chapter 4). Now their complete failure to agree on a common approach to deal with the aggressive ambitions of Mussolini and of Hitler robbed the League of any remaining claim to be able to maintain international peace through collective action. After the failure to protect Abyssinia against Italian aggression its credibility was completely destroyed. 'New League methods' were now discarded in favour of 'old diplomacy' which sanctioned the absorption of Austria by Germany in March 1938, and negotiated the Munich Agreement in the autumn of that year. Czechoslovakia and Austria, together with Albania, disappeared, just as Abyssinia had done, and before long, war broke out once again in Europe in September 1939, when German troops invaded Poland. Ironically, just as the League's influence was waning, in 1937 it finally moved into purpose-built accommodation idyllically sited by the shores of Lake Geneva.

One last act remained for the League to perform. Stalin had concluded a non-aggression pact with Hitler in August, 1939, and three months later Soviet troops invaded Finland in an act of unprovoked aggression. The League Council was hastily summoned, and seven of its 14 members resolved to expel the Soviet Union from the League, with no member opposed – the only time in the League's history that this course of action was taken. And with the expulsion of the Soviet Union, the League ensured that it would not survive beyond the Second World War, as Stalin, together with Roosevelt and Churchill, worked to construct an entirely new international body to regulate the post-war world.

8

The League and the Development of International Society

The League undoubtedly failed in its main task of preventing the outbreak of another global military conflict. Yet, at the same time, it achieved considerable success across a wide range of economic, social and humanitarian endeavours, and helped to create a global international network of experts, voluntary international organisations, private foundations and international civil servants. The League was housed in Geneva, initially at the Hotel National and from the mid 1930s in a specially designed building beside Lake Geneva, the Palais des Nations. The League Assembly, on which all members were represented, met every year in the autumn; from its first meeting in 1920, people and organisations from all over the world flocked to observe the proceedings and lobby the delegates. While the League Assembly was never able to live up to its most ardent supporters' expectations that it would become a 'People's Parliament', the accessibility of its meetings and the wide publicity which they attracted had a global impact, and provided both a focus for existing groups and charities and a stimulus for the creation of new bodies and networks. By the late 1920s, the League's Hand-book of International Organisations listed 560 private inter-national bodies, and there were also some 40 national League of Nations societies, which were members of an International Federation of League of Nations Societies based in Brussels.[1] As we saw in Chapter 6 in relation to the Abyssinian crisis, there was a very active League of Nations Union in Britain, with more than 3,000 branches meeting regularly and with a monthly publication, *Headway*, that had a circulation of more than 100,000 copies, undoubtedly reaching a reader-ship of many thousands more.[2] Millions of people across the world, in religious, cultural, humanitarian or social networks, identified with the League and with its activities, contributing to the emergence, for the first time, of 'a global sense of "humanity"'.[3]

The creation and development of a strong League Secre-tariat, drawn from over 30 countries including the United States, greatly assisted in this development. One of the most innovative aspects of the League's establishment was its high-quality secretariat organised along the lines of an inter-national civil service. The first Secretary-General, Sir Eric Drummond, brought to the League the high standards and the impartiality of his British civil service experience, and sought to ensure that League officials were responsible to, and owed their loyalty to, the League and the international community rather than to their national governments. While he was not always successful, the League Secretariat – which grew steadily to more than 600 officials at its peak – became respected across the globe for the quality of its work and its expertise. It was organised into five sections covering health-care, economic and financial co-operation, the care and set-tlement of refugees, minorities' issues and disarmament.

Each of these areas of work expanded in remit extensively in the two decades after 1920. The accumulation of information, expertise and detailed statistics on a wide variety of important issues made the League the focal point of up-to-date research and findings on current crises and emerging global problems. Its conferences drew to Geneva and to other major cities hundreds of participants and international experts from all over the world, including from non-member countries such as the United States and, before 1934, Soviet Russia. The role of the Secretary-General became increasingly important, although the position was occupied by two very different personalities in Sir Eric Drummond and his successor, the French official Joseph Avenol.[4] The League, as the centre of a worldwide network of administrative, technical, humanitarian, economic and financial expertise, built up a legacy which was far too valuable to be allowed to disappear, despite its failures as a peacekeeping body. In recognition of how important and far-reaching the League's work in these areas had been, its successor body – the United Nations – built on its foundations, and particularly on the organisation and work of the League Secretariat.

Under the peace treaties of 1919 and 1920, the League Secretariat was given the task of carrying out a range of specific administrative responsibilities arising from the peace settlement, relating to issues which had proved particularly contentious at the Paris Peace Conference. The first two concerned the Saar district and the area around the city and port of Danzig, which were parts of Germany until 1918. The Saar basin was rich in coalfields and other mineral resources, which the French claimed as compensation for the wanton destruction of French coalfields by the German army during the war. While it was agreed at Paris that the French should be granted ownership of the mines, there was considerable disagreement about the governance of the Saar area. The compromise finally reached, after much argument, was that Germany should cede sovereignty of the area to the League, which would govern it for 15 years, after which time a plebiscite would be held to ask the inhabitants whether they wished to return to Germany, transfer to France or continue with the League regime.[5]

There was, particularly in the early years of the 1920s, inevitable friction between the inhabitants of the Saar and the Governing Commission set up by the League, particularly during the French occupation of the Ruhr area of Germany in 1923. There were repeated complaints of undue French pressure on the Governing Commission, and of French attempts to go beyond the permitted exploitation of mineral resources and to try to engage the Saarlanders in a range of pro-French political activities. Nonetheless, the area remained largely peaceful and efficiently run until 1935, when the inhabitants voted overwhelmingly to return to German rule, a result greeted with enormous fanfare by Hitler and the Nazi regime in Germany.

Danzig was another area which was in dispute, this time between the peacemakers and the new Polish state. It was a crucial element in the thirteenth of Woodrow Wilson's Fourteen Points, promising Poland 'free and secure access to the sea'. However, it was a largely German city, which Lloyd George in particular was reluctant to see under Polish rule. The compromise reached was to establish Danzig as a free city under the administration of the League of Nations, but with economic links to Poland.[6] Thus for twenty years, its day-to-day operations were conducted under the watchful eye of a specially appointed League High Commissioner who reported regularly to Geneva. As with the Saar, there was continuous friction, this time between the Polish government and the Danzig city officials, and after 1933 with the Nazi government in Germany. Tensions in the city and allegations of discrimination against German inhabitants, fanned by the Nazi propaganda put out by vociferous party members, rose markedly in the mid-to-late 1930s. Yet Danzig remained relatively peaceful and was well governed by the League until the summer of 1939, when Hitler's resolve to reabsorb both it and the Polish Corridor into the German Third Reich triggered the outbreak of European war.

The reports from the Saar and Danzig were closely scrutinised both by the League Secretariat and by the League Council, and issues arising from them were regularly debated by League members. Thus, despite the political, economic and geographical complexities of both regimes, the League was undoubtedly successful in its administrative supervisory role, and set a standard of impartial governance that was built on by the United Nations after the Second World War.

An even more daunting challenge to the League contained in the treaties of peace and subsequent agreements was the protection of minority peoples in countries which had emerged from the war with disputed boundaries or as newly constituted states. By 1920, there were 30 million people in Eastern and Central Europe living in states in which they were not the dominant nationality. One of the concerns of the peacemakers in Paris had been to protect the rights of the Jewish communities scattered throughout Eastern Europe. This protection was then extended to a wide range of minority populations left on the wrong sides of national borders, in the hope that a system of guaranteed rights would reconcile them to their new countries.[7] The League found itself with responsibility to ensure that these rights were upheld in 16 very different countries: Poland, Czechoslovakia, Romania, Yugoslavia, Greece, Albania, Austria, Hungary, Bulgaria, Lithuania, Finland in respect of the Aland Islands, Germany in respect of Upper Silesia, and later Latvia, Estonia, Turkey and Iraq.

Inevitably, minority protection proved to be a thankless task for the League. There were continuing protests on the part of governments and complaints by minorities that their grievances were being ignored. The League, as with the supervision of the Saar and Danzig, took its responsibilities very seriously, and Council members spent inordinate amounts of time studying petitions from aggrieved minorities, taking up complaints and trying to negotiate changes with increasingly hostile governments. As Walters observed, the League's work in this area was 'difficult and invidious', and though in general terms most minority people were protected from severe injustice and harm, the governments under scrutiny resented being singled out in this way for continual surveillance of their activities and criticism of their policies.[8] As a result, in many areas, tensions between ethnic groups escalated, though prior to 1939 serious violence was largely contained. However, after the appalling genocide and wholesale slaughter of minorities which occurred during the Second World War, it was felt that a different approach by the new United Nations was needed. Minority protection through a system of petitions, as carried out by the League, had patently not been effective, but efforts to build on one aspect of this work – enabling individuals to make legitimate complaints against the regimes under which they were living – led to the development of a new system of individual 'human rights'. In 1948, the Universal Declaration of Human Rights was issued under the auspices of the

United Nations, followed in 1950 by the Council of Europe's Human Rights Convention. By the 1960s the European Court of Human Rights, set up in 1959, was enabling individuals to take up cases against sovereign states.[9] Thus even though the League's work with regard to protecting minorities had been difficult and largely unsuccessful, it had provided useful evidence to help shape a different approach after the Second World War.

A fourth task given to the League by the peacemakers was to oversee the administration of the former German colonies and Turkish territories which were seized by the Allied powers during the First World War. Article 22 of the League Covenant divided these into three categories – A, B and C – depending on their geographical situation, their economic condition and the stage of development of their inhabitants. The allocation of mandates and the terms on which they were to be carried out caused bitter arguments amongst the victorious allies Britain, France and Japan; the British Dominions, particularly South Africa and Australia; and President Wilson.[10] These were finally assigned by the Supreme Council between 1919 and 1921, with the designated Mandatory Powers receiving 'full powers of legislation and administration', but with the obligation to furnish annual reports on their stewardship to a League Commission which was made up of 11 experts in colonial affairs.

Cynics both at the time and since have sneered that the system of mandates was simply annexation of the spoils of war masquerading as enlightened humanitarianism. Certainly, the way in which some Mandatory Powers exercised their responsibilities – particularly South Africa's administration of South West Africa (the territory now known as Namibia) – gave some credence to this charge. And yet the ideals which lay at the heart of the new system and aimed to distinguish it from colonial rule – that mandatory rule should be 'for the well-being and development of less advanced people' and that it should form a 'sacred mission for civilisation' – exercised a growing influence in the inter-war period. The League Commissioners were for the most part men with considerable knowledge of colonial rule, having experienced it at first hand or written extensively about it. They took their duties seriously and forced the Mandatory Powers to justify and modify their policies in many areas by commenting in detail on their reports, and questioning their governors robustly, often at great length. The Mandatory Powers soon discovered that they could not operate unilaterally, however much they would have liked to, and had to demonstrate in their annual reports how they were upholding the principles of mandatory rule in their territories. Furthermore, from 1923, it was agreed that inhabitants in mandated areas could send petitions to the Mandates Commission on matters that might be alleged to breach the terms of the mandate. International societies, in particular the long-established Anti-Slavery Society, were very active in encouraging native peoples to articulate their grievances, and to do so in a way which would conform to the criteria for petitions laid down by the League Secretariat.

As a result, some 3,000 petitions were received by the League Secretariat at Geneva in the ensuing decade and a half. The great majority of them related to problems in Syria and in Palestine, but over 100 concerned grievances in South West Africa. These petitions were discussed by the Mandates Commission, circulated to member states and publicised across the globe. In this way, people living in mandated territories were given a distinct voice, and their concerns were not simply dealt with as in the colonies – by an uncaring, unresponsive, omnipotent colonial power – but were discussed at an international level, with the mandated power having to respond to the charges.[11]

The bulk of the protests came from the A-mandated areas – Syria, Iraq and Palestine – and in 1932 the British government agreed to terminate its mandate over Iraq and support its admission to the League as a sovereign state. However, another British-mandated area, Palestine, experienced mounting tensions and outbreaks of violence in the mid-to-late 1930s as Arabs and Jews battled for supremacy, and it eventually freed itself from British control in controversial circumstances in 1948. The other A-mandated areas were all recognised as sovereign states soon after the end of the Second World War, while the remaining mandates were transferred to the Trusteeship Council, a new body established under the United Nations. While this body consisted of government representatives rather than independent experts, it built on the work of the League's Mandates Commission, and, over the ensuing decades, supervised the transition of the mandated areas to statehood.[12] Looking back now from the 21st century, we can see how transformational the mandates system proved to be, not just for the areas under its supervision, but for that half of the globe which, immediately after the First World War, was still in a state of colonial dependency. The mandates system, as written, posed 'uncomfortable questions about empire all over the world', and mandatory rule contained within itself 'a presumption of independence and thus an implicit expiry date'.[13] As Susan Pederson has argued, the mandates system was a 'vehicle for internationalism', providing a mechanism by which a set of colonial issues were displaced from the national or imperial arena to the international stage. In this way, the League brought about a 'geopolitical transformation' through the mandates system, and helped to make the end of empire imaginable. It unleashed 'a force that could not be contained', mobilised new constituencies, generated new claims, established new practices and 'articulated new norms'.[14]

Article 23 of the League Covenant committed the League to undertake a broad range of humanitarian activities, and article 24 placed under its direction all existing international bureaux dealing with a whole host of miscellaneous issues which had become the subject of international regulation before 1914. In some areas, therefore, the League had solid foundations on which to build; in others it had to improvise, and its work was shaped by the nature of the humanitarian crises which arose in war-torn Europe. One area of concern which had not been identified in the League Covenant but which came to the fore in the immediate post-war years was the large number of stateless refugees fleeing the civil war in Russia and the fighting still raging in some parts of Eastern and south-eastern Europe. To begin with, giving them help and trying to resettle them was seen as an urgent but tempo-rary task, and was organised through a Refugee Organisation, run with tireless zeal by a celebrated Norwegian explorer, Fridtjof Nansen, who was appointed High Commissioner for refugees. In 1921–2, Nansen and his three assistants managed to return nearly 500,000 men from Russia, with help from the Red Cross and other agencies, and the creation of a 'Nansen passport' enabled about 90,000 stateless refugees to settle in new areas. However, the flow of displaced people continued throughout the inter-war period and the work of assisting them proved to be an intractable and unending task for the League's Refugee Organisation. Nansen died in 1930, and his work was continued thereafter by a new body, the Nansen Office for Refugees, which had to face the challenges of a wave of largely Jewish refugees from Germany after 1933, from the Saar in 1935, and then from Austria and Czechoslovakia in the late 1930s, as well as trying to help those fleeing from Fascist Italy, Spain and the increasingly brutal Stalinist regime in Russia. Despite inordinate difficulties, disputes with individual governments and a perennial shortage of funds, the League's work of helping refugees and displaced persons continued during and immediately after the Second World War, until 1948 when its operations were merged into the new International Refugee Organisation set up by the United Nations.[15]

Assisting refugees and displaced people might not have been one of the tasks spelled out in the Covenant, but it proved to be one of the League's most significant and enduring legacies. A recent assessment of the League's work in this area argues that 'the League, more than any other single international institution in the 20th century, founded an international system to deal with the challenge posed to nation states by refugees. It created a regime based on asylum, assistance and burden sharing that continues to this day.'[16] And this theme, of the importance of the League's work in laying the foundations for the significant expansion and progress which occurred in the second half of the 20th century under the aegis of the United Nations, is reflected across a range of humanitarian and economic activities. The League's Health Organisation from its inception carried out a wide variety of tasks across the world. It worked to combat and to try to control the spread of a range of dangerous epidemics such as typhus, cholera, smallpox and yellow fever, and its experts studied tropical diseases in Africa. It organised specialised conferences, oversaw trials of new drugs and helped to develop new vaccines. Its remit expanded to cover public health, nutrition, the quality of food and water and rural hygiene. And its work was greatly assisted by generous charitable donations, notably from the American Rockefeller Foundation, which gave the League over $500,000 for its international health work.[17] The United States may not have been a member of the League, but it took an active role in its humanitarian work, with American representatives sitting on a range of the League's expert health and social committees. Within 20 years, the Health Organisation was working across the globe at a number of different levels, ranging from pioneering medical research to assistance for remote rural communities in dealing with the problems of everyday life. After the Second World War, it provided the foundation for the World Health Organisation, established under the auspices of the United Nations.

The League's work to combat the traffic in opium and other dangerous drugs, while extensive, was less successful. Though detailed statistics on the nature and extent of the traffic were collected and published, revealing its significant extent, combatting the scourge proved to be much more difficult. There were ongoing attempts to limit the manufacture of narcotic drugs and the cultivation of the poppy, but no great success had been achieved by 1939. More noteworthy was the work to try to prevent the trafficking of women and children which involved League officials and experts in a range of sensitive issues. Individual states, particularly those less economically and socially developed, resented such outside interference, but nonetheless progress was recorded, in the shape of the raising of the age of consent and of the age of marriage in a number of countries, and the abolition of licensed brothels in most countries where they existed. Less successful were attempts to halt the white slave traffic, but even here the League's work left its mark. One historian has argued that the League's campaign against white slavery was a major stepping stone in the development of an international human rights regime.[18]

While such humanitarian activities were specifically item-ised in the League Covenant, little was spelled out in relation to economic or financial issues in which the League might involve itself. But in the post-war period, with victor and van-quished powers alike facing the crippling financial and eco-nomic costs of the Great War, the League Secretariat devoted increasing resources to help promote economic recovery, which would then hopefully contribute to political stability. The first challenge arose in connection with Austria, which was struggling to survive after the collapse of the Habsburg Empire. By 1922, this newly constituted state was in debt, and faced massive inflation of around 3,000 per cent and high reparation payments. Its population – a third of it crowded into the capital, Vienna – was starving. Without external help, disaster loomed. League experts were mobilised, and within a few months, working with Austrian officials and a network of external financiers and bankers, they were able to agree on a package of economic assistance in the form of a £26 million loan financed by the raising of private capital in the United States money markets. A loan of some £10 million for neigh-bouring Hungary soon followed, and the budgets of both countries were placed under international supervision, under the watchful eye of a Commissioner General appointed by the League. With stringent controls in place, the currencies of the two countries were stabilised, their budgets were balanced and their economies were strengthened. Economic assistance to Greece, Bulgaria and Estonia followed; the networks of officials and experts created as a result of dealing with these crises then facilitated wider economic assistance in the shape of the Dawes and later Young plans to deal with German reparations and Allied war debts.[19] Given the political and economic fragility of much of Central and Eastern Europe in the 1920s, such League intervention was crucial in helping to promote stability. As one official in the British Foreign Office commented, it stopped Central and Eastern European states from 'throwing up their hands and going Bolshy'.[20] And, as with its humanitarian work, the League could count on American co-operation and financial support through informal networks of experts and officials. This was invaluable at a time when the governments of the United States, Britain, France and Germany were locked in arguments and disputes about inter-Allied debts and reparation payments.[21]

The League's financial and economic work was carried out by an Economic Committee and a Financial Committee, each composed of 12 members appointed by the League Council. They were chosen for their expertise rather than for their nationality, and were a mixture of government officials, economic experts and bank directors. In turn, they relied on the assistance of the officials in the League's economic and financial section, and by 1930 their number had grown to 56. To begin with, they had focused on collecting and comparing a range of statistics and collating economic intelligence from around the globe, which they presented to the two League specialist committees and issued to League members. But their activities widened and became more ambitious. In 1927 a World Economic Conference was convened at Geneva, attracting 194 national delegates and 226 world trade and finance experts, not just drawn from League member states but including also the United States and Russia. Its agenda of promoting economic and monetary co-operation across the globe made it, in Patricia Clavin's words, the 'first economic conference in history with global reach'.[22] The onset of the global depression after 1929 greatly hampered such efforts, but another World Economic Conference was convened in London in 1933 to try to deal collectively with its impact. Some 65 states were represented, of which ten were non-members of the League, and there were more than 1,000 delegates. The conference's opening ceremony was broadcast around the world; alas, it proved difficult to reach any agreement on the intractable economic and financial problems facing the world. Even so, the economic and financial section of the League was the most active and fast-growing element of the secretariat in the 1930s, enquiring into a range of issues, working with economists from around the world to seek the causes of the depression and try to agree on possible solutions, and attempting to combat the growing tide of protectionist economic policies. Much of this work inspired and fed into the creation, at the end of the Second World War, of the World Bank and the International Monetary Fund. Furthermore, the League's emphasis on the importance of international trade co-operation to promote both political harmony and economic growth fed through into the General Agreement on Tariffs and Trade, negotiated in 1947, and into the establishment of the European Coal and Steel Community. By the late 1930s, the League's social, economic and financial activities had extended to every part of the globe, and a committee under the chairmanship of a former Australian Prime Minister, Stanley Bruce, recommended that they should be brought together rather than being pursued by distinct sections and committees of the League. The Bruce

Report argued that a new Central Committee for Economic and Social Questions should be established, and made open to non-member states. The outbreak of war postponed this development, but it took shape in 1946 as the Economic and Social Council of the United Nations. One result of bringing together economic, social, financial and health work was to pave the way for schemes of international development, which proliferated in the decades after the Second World War.[23]

Brief mention must be made of the League's pioneering work in the field of intellectual co-operation, which was carried out by a committee of 12, and later 15, eminent scholars who included Marie Curie, Albert Einstein, Henri Bergson and Gilbert Murray. Its main aim was to increase contacts between teachers, artists, scientists and authors, and thereby to strengthen the likelihood of international harmony and peace by forging a true 'rapprochement between peoples'. There was a particular desire to emphasise the benefits of intellectual co-operation for young people.[24] Unfortunately, a number of its initiatives proved to be impracticable, and there was a lot of disagreement amongst its leading intellectual lights, while funding was tightly controlled by the League Assembly.[25] Nonetheless, much of the committee's work was continued after the war by the United Nations Educational, Scientific and Cultural Organisation (UNESCO) under United Nations auspices.

Finally, mention must be made of two important League bodies which after 1945 were transferred virtually unaltered from the League to the United Nations. The International Labour Organisation (ILO) was established by the Treaty of Versailles, and its constitution was included in each of the subsequent peace treaties concluded at Paris. It was to operate under the aegis of the League, which provided its finances, but to be administered as an independent organisation through a Governing Body and a Labour Office. Its remit was to ensure just and humane conditions of labour in the countries of its member states, and to promote the physical, moral and intellectual well-being of industrial wage earners – an objective which was seen to be crucially important in the early 1920s in keeping workers away from the clutches of revolutionary Marxist and Bolshevik agitators.

It operated through a tripartite governing structure which consisted of representatives of governments, employers and workers. Its director until 1932 was Albert Thomas, an energetic and committed French socialist, and under his leadership the ILO flourished and pursued its aims vigorously through conferences and the adoption of labour conventions, with a particular focus on the protection of women and child workers and trying to secure an eight-hour working day. Germany and Austria were admitted as members in 1920, and states who subsequently withdrew from the League – such as Brazil and Japan – chose to remain in the organisation. Thomas died in 1932, but was succeeded by his able British deputy, Harold Butler, and as the League's peacekeeping activities went into eclipse in the later 1930s, the ILO continued to be strongly supported by its member states, and particularly by the union representatives operating on behalf of industrial workers. In 1938, the United States joined the ILO, and after the outbreak of war in Europe the organisation moved its headquarters from Geneva to Montreal. With the establishment of the United Nations, the ILO became one of its specialist agencies, and continued with its mission, operating virtually unchanged to the present day.

The Permanent Court of International Justice, established

under article 14 of the League Covenant, started work in the Peace Palace at the Hague in 1922. Nine judges and four Deputy Judges were elected jointly by the Council and Assembly during the second League Assembly meeting on the grounds of their legal eminence and ability to 'represent the main forms of civilisation and the principal legal systems of the world'. They were kept busy from the outset, either in giving advisory opinions to the Council or in deciding cases submitted to the Court by individual governments. The Court's reputation and authority grew steadily as the years went by.[26] Between 1922 and 1939 it heard 66 cases, of which 28 were requests for an advisory opinion. Its 'optional clause', whereby member states who signed up to it agreed to be bound by its jurisdiction in classes of disputes deemed to be 'justiciable', was taken up by 40 countries, including Britain in 1929. By 1939 nearly 600 international agreements contained a clause referring to its jurisdiction. Its success showed the important role that a standing international court could play 'in promoting orderly international relations in conditions where there was already a strong international desire for order' and it established a 'significant landmark in the gradual acceptance by states that rules had a place in international politics'.[27] The International Court of Justice, set up after the Second World War by the United Nations, reproduced in almost identical form the League's Permanent Court of International Justice, and has continued to extend its authority and increase its profile in recent years.

It is therefore clear that in a wide range of humanitarian, social, economic and legal areas the League was an important pioneering body, laying strong foundations for advances in the second half of the 20th century. We can see much more clearly now, as the centenary of its birth approaches, the global reach of its work and the transformational effect of so many of its programmes. It is not surprising, therefore, that recent scholarship in this field has emphasised the importance of weighing the success and impact of the League's social, technical and humanitarian work alongside its more trumpeted peacekeeping failures. As Patricia Clavin observed, the League served as 'an incubator for ideas and practices that continue to shape the 21st-century world'.[28] Its activities contributed directly to the emergence of an interconnected global network of not just governments but voluntary groups, experts and charitable foundations. We can see the emergence of 'international society' in this inter-war period, and the League was instrumental in bringing it about. Considered from this perspective, the success of the League is undoubtable, and this explains why, even before the end of the war which it failed to prevent, a new body bearing a strong resemblance to the League was established.

9

The League is Dead: Long Live the United Nations

The outline of a new world organisation was agreed in the midst of the Second World War by the wartime allies the United States, the USSR and Britain. While the intention was to construct a very different international body from the League, according to a British diplomat who had been based at Geneva in the 1930s, the nascent United Nations bore 'a most embarrassing resemblance to its predecessor. Again and again, without any direct reference to what had transpired during twenty years at Geneva, we arrived, surprisingly, at results that might seem to have been modelled on the earlier organisation'.[1] The United Nations was to operate through two main bodies, a Security Council and a General Assembly, and to be administered by an international secretariat under an independent Secretary-General. It was to be an organisation of sovereign states, all of which retained jurisdiction over their domestic affairs, and to have a wide range of responsibilities and agencies designed both to maintain peace and to improve the general welfare of its members. One lesson learned from the League was that issues relating to international peace and security had to be interwoven with economic, financial and social concerns – and that, in promoting international stability, the United Nations and its agencies needed to focus less on the purely political and more on the 'economic, cultural and social'.[2]

But there were some important differences that reveal what the framers of the United Nations Charter in 1946 believed to be the major flaws in the structure and operation of the League which they were determined to avoid. First and foremost, the United Nations was created as a free-standing organisation not linked to a peace treaty, and was not therefore seen as the guardian of the post–Second World War territorial settlement. Secondly, its Security Council was to be based unequivocally on the Great Powers working together in concert, each of them able to exercise a veto on any proposed action – precisely the kind of powerful driving force the British government in 1919 had wanted the League Council to be. As the British commentary on the United Nations Charter pointed out, 'the successful working of the United Nations depends on the preservation of the unanimity of the Great Powers .... If this unanimity is seriously undermined no provision of the Charter is likely to be of much avail'.[3]

The task of the five permanent members of the Security Council – the United States, the USSR, Britain, France and nationalist China – was to work together to secure the maintenance of international peace and security, and to this end they could take decisions by majority vote which were binding on all members of the United Nations. Thus as a last resort, the Security Council could take action to enforce peace, including the use of military force if arbitration and sanctions failed – something the French government had in

1919 urged in vain that the League should be equipped to do. The reason for this change was very clear. In 1919, both the British and American governments aimed to construct a body which would prevent conflict from spreading by creating mechanisms to deal with sudden and unexpected outbreaks of military aggression rather than with premeditated military expansion. After 1945, the United Nations was equipped to deal with planned aggression masterminded and launched by determined and power-hungry dictators and despots. It would indeed be fair to say that, whereas the League was established to prevent the First World War from breaking out again, the United Nations was set up to combat the aggressive territorial expansion which caused the outbreak of the Second World War, and thus its Security Council was given far greater powers than the League had possessed.

The division of powers and responsibilities between the Security Council and the General Assembly was also much more clearly delineated than had been the case with the League. The Security Council's remit was to work for peace and security through collective action and diplomacy; all other issues, whether economic, social or relating to general welfare, were deemed to be matters of common concern and therefore the responsibility of the General Assembly to deal with through majority voting. Unlike the binding decisions of the Security Council, resolutions of the General Assembly were to be recommendations which would not commit member states to action.

The most obvious difference between the two bodies was the inclusion in the United Nations of all the world's leading powers, particularly the United States and the USSR. Their absence from the League had crippled it from the outset, but as these two principal victors emerged from the Second World

War, they were determined to drive forward the new international body which they had created. This inevitably meant that from the start the United Nations had the global reach which the League had struggled to achieve, symbolised by the fact that its headquarters were established in New York.

Thus the United Nations was framed to capitalise on the League's successes and avoid its deficiencies. Even so, it has not operated as effectively as its founders anticipated. It was hampered and then divided by the growing antagonism between the capitalist United States and the communist USSR, which undermined the effectiveness of the United Nations as the Cold War took hold. After the establishment of a communist regime under Mao Tse-tung in mainland China, it took more than two decades before an agreement was reached that it should replace the nationalist Chinese regime of Taiwan on the Security Council. As worldwide political engagement became more difficult in the Cold War era, there was a proliferation of new international technical, economic and financial agencies – especially those focusing on policies of development – which increasingly had only a loose connection with the main United Nations institutions. Nonetheless, the United Nations remains a cornerstone of global international collaboration, with 193 current member states, including all the world's most powerful countries. It has pioneered new approaches to counter aggression, such as through its peacekeeping activities, and its Secretary-Generals have become leading international figures. Significant problems remain, such as trying to achieve Great Power unanimity when crises erupt, endeavouring to curb the spread of nuclear weapons and trying to ensure that member states observe their international human rights obligations, but the United Nations' success in presiding over and facilitating international change has been greater than what the League was able to achieve.

Lord Cecil claimed in 1946 that, 'But for the great experiment of the League, the United Nations could never have come into existence. The fundamental principles of the Charter and the Covenant are the same and it is gratifying to some of us that, after the violent controversies that have raged for the last quarter of a century, it is now generally accepted that peace can be secured only by international co-operation, broadly on the lines agreed to in 1920.'[4] The League was indeed a 'great experiment', and after nearly a century we can now clearly see that it was in its way a pioneering organisation, laying the foundations for our global and increasingly interconnected world. As we have seen, in many areas of activity it achieved great success, but it was hampered by three major difficulties. In the first place, it operated in an extremely unstable international environment which generated a level of political and economic turbulence that was bound to undermine the League's effectiveness. Secondly, in the absence of the United States and Russia, it was driven by two Great Powers, Britain and France, whose world influence and global reach was on the wane and who were fatally divided in their views on how the League could most effectively maintain international peace. And thirdly, the First World War had fatally weakened the economic strength and political dominance of its European combatants and had accelerated a decisive shift of world power which was already occurring before 1914. The League was conceived as a worldwide organisation, but its engine was in practice powered from Europe, and it was not strong enough to promote peace across the globe.

And yet its ideals, striving for the establishment of a

peaceful community of states all agreeing to abide by a clear set of rules of conduct, remained powerful and evoked strong popular support. Smaller states relished the democratic structure of the League Assembly, where once a year they could give their views on the conduct and behaviour of the Great Powers. The League helped to bring into existence a 'different dynamic of international co-operation' and those who worked on its behalf began to craft that 'network of norms and agreements by which our world is [now] regulated, if not quite governed'. It was not able to fulfil the ambitious aspirations of its founders or the exaggerated hopes of its most fervent supporters, but it was the world's first 'sustained and consequential experiment in internationalism', a significant and exploratory first phase which paved the way for a second, more effective period of international collaboration under the United Nations.[5] Rather than dwell on its weaknesses or condemn its failures, we should applaud its successes while continuing to learn important lessons from its history.

Notes

1: One Vision – Many Approaches

1. See, for example, Daniel Patrick Moynihan, *Pandaemonium: Ethnicity in International Politics* (Oxford University Press: 1993) pp 9, 78.

2 W Kuehl, *The United States and International Organisation to 1920* (Vanderbilt University Press: 1969) p 32.

3. F S Northedge, *The League of Nations: Its Life and Times 1920 – 46* (Leicester University Press: 1986) p 15.

4. Kuehl, *The United States and International Organisation*, pp 156 –7.

5. Kuehl, *The United States and International Organisation*, p 141.

6. A Zimmern, *The League of Nations and the Rule of Law, 1918 – 1935* (Macmillan and Co: 1936) p 114.

7. Kuehl, *The United States and International Organisation*, p 81.

8. Kuehl, *The United States and International Organisation*, p 127.

9. Kuehl, *The United States and International Organisation*, p 89.

10. Zimmern, *The League of Nations and the Rule of Law*, pp 128–31.

11. Zimmern, *The League of Nations and the Rule of Law*, pp 166–9.

12. Kuehl, *The United States and International Organisation*, pp 190–1.

13. Kuehl, *The United States and International Organisation*, p 214.

14. Kuehl, *The United States and International Organisation*, p 225.

15. Zimmern, *The League of Nations and the Rule of Law*, pp 217–18.

16. R Henig (ed), *The League of Nations* (Oliver and Boyd: 1973) p 24.

17. Henig (ed), *The League of Nations*, p 22.

18. Henig (ed), *The League of Nations*, pp 25–8.

19. Henig (ed), *The League of Nations*, pp 28–32.

20. Kuehl, *The United States and International Organisation*, p 255.

21. Northedge, *The League of Nations: Its Life and Times*, pp 30–1.

22. Northedge, *The League of Nations: Its Life and Times*, pp 31–3.

23. Kuehl, *The United States and International Organisation*, p 263; House, diary 15 Aug 1918, cited in C Seymour, *The Intimate Papers of Colonel House* (Ernest Benn: 1928) Vol IV, pp 48–50; see also pp 27–38. Hereafter Seymour, *Intimate Papers of Colonel House*.

24. Arno J Mayer, *Politics and Diplomacy of Peacemaking* (Weidenfeld and Nicolson: 1968) p 177.

2: The Drafting of the Covenant, Paris, 1919

1. House, diary entry 4 Nov 1918, in Seymour, *Intimate Papers of Colonel House,* Vol IV p 186.
2. J. Smuts, 'Our Policy at the Peace Conference', 3 December 1918, FO 371/3451.
3. Lord Riddell, *Intimate Diary of the Peace Conference and After* (Victor Gollancz: 1933) p 7, hereafter Riddell, *Intimate Diary.*
4. Riddell, *Intimate Diary,* 19 Feb 1921, p 279
5. G W Egerton, *Great Britain and the Creation of the League of Nations* (Scholar Press: 1979) p 117, hereafter Egerton, *Great Britain.*
6. Lord Robert Cecil, diary entry, 29 Jan 1919, Cecil Papers 51131.
7. Egerton, *Great Britain,* pp 119–120.
8. Trevor Wilson (ed), *The Political Diaries of C.P. Scott, 1911–1928* (Collins: 1970) pp 370–1, Hereafter Wilson (ed), *C.P. Scott Diaries.*
9. Lord Robert Cecil, diary entry, 22 Jan 1919.
10. Seymour, *Intimate Papers of Colonel House,* Vol IV, pp 313–14.
11. S Bonsal, *Unfinished Business* (Michael Joseph: 1944) pp 32–3.
12. Zimmern, *The League of Nations and the Rule of Law,* p 241; Egerton, *Great Britain,* pp 131–2.
13. A Sharp, *The Versailles Settlement: Peacemaking in Paris, 1919* (Macmillan: 1991) p 57, hereafter A Sharp, *The Versailles Settlement.*
14. S Bonsal, *Unfinished Business,* pp 48–9. See also Zimmern, *The League of Nations and the Rule of Law,* pp 247–50; and Egerton, *Great Britain,* p 136.
15. Bonsal, *Unfinished Business,* p 49.

16. Egerton, *Great Britain*, p 135.
17. Northedge, *The League of Nations: Its Life and Times*, pp 44–5.
18. FRUS, Paris Peace Conference 1919, III, pp 215–16.
19. Egerton, *Great Britain*, pp 141–9.
20. Egerton, *Great Britain*, p 161.
21. Lord Robert Cecil, diary entry, 26 Mar 1919.
22. David Hunter Miller, *My Diary at the Conference of Paris, with Documents* 21 vols (Appeal Printing Co.: 1924–6).
23. S Roskill, *Hankey, Man of Secrets* (Collins: 1972) Vol II, pp 79–80; S D Waley, *Edwin Montagu* (Asia Publishing House: 1964).
24. Imperial War Conference, 24 December 1918, Cab 23/42.
25. Henig (ed), *League of Nations*, p 10. Balfour was chairing a meeting to discuss the Draft Treaty of Mutual Assistance, 19 Feb 1924.
26. Lord Grey, *Twenty Five Years, 1892–1916* (Hodder and Stoughton: 1928) Vol I, pp 91–2. Barnes, 14 Feb 1919 in D Hunter Miller, *The Drafting of the Covenant* (GP Putnam's Sons: 1928) Vol II, pp 574–5.
27. Hunter Miller, *The Drafting of the Covenant*, Vol I, pp 41–4; Foreign Office Memorandum of December 1918 quoted in Zimmern, *The League of Nations and the Rule of Law*, p 198. Egerton, *Great Britain*, p 172.
28. Wilson (ed), *C. P. Scott Diaries*, p 374; Egerton, *Great Britain*, p 165.
29. Margaret Macmillan, *Peacemakers: The Paris Conference of 1919 and Its Attempt to End War* (John Murray: 2001) p 106.
30. House of Commons, 16 Apr 1919; House of Commons, 21 Jul 1919.

31. Philip Kerr, 'Europe, the Covenant and the Protocol, *Round Table* (March 1925) (see list of articles in J R M Butler, *Lord Lothian 1882 – 1940* [Macmillan and Co: 1960]).

32. Plenary session of Paris Peace Conference, 14 Feb 1919, quoted in Egerton, *Great Britain*, pp 139 – 140.

3: A Faltering Start

1. Egerton, *Great Britain*, p 180.

2. Documents on British Foreign Policy (1st Series) Vol V, pp 366, 4 Oct 1919, hereafter DBFP.

3. DBFP Vol V, pp 399, 430.

4. DBFP Vol VI, pp 1054–5.

5. Sir Maurice Hankey, *Diplomacy by Conference. Studies in public affairs, 1920–1946* (Ernest Benn: 1946) – a lecture delivered to the Institute of International Affairs and later published as the first of a collection of essays under the same title.

6. Comment by Lord Hardinge, F.O. 371/4313.

7. *The Times*, 26 May 1921. It reported the vote as being 56–30, and attributed the low turn-out to the impending Tripos Examinations.

8. Verbatim records of Imperial Conference 1921, Cab 32/3; W Kuehl and Dunn, *American Internationalists and the League of Nations 1920–39* (Kent State University Press: 1997) p 18, hereafter Kuehl and Dunn, *American Internationalists and the League of Nations*.

9. Geddes to Lloyd George, 17 March 1921, Lloyd George Papers F 60/4/16.

10. Guest to Lloyd George, 4 October 1929, Lloyd George Papers F 22/3/29.

11. F P Walters, *A History of the League of Nations* (Oxford University Press: 1952), hereafter Walters, *A History of the League of Nations*.

12. Conversation between Lloyd George and M de Karnebeek at Genoa, 2 May 1922, Cab 21/239.

13. Curzon to Imperial Conference, 8 July 1921, Cab 32/2 part I.

14. Riddell, *Intimate Diary*, p 255.

15. By 1926, individual membership had increased to 600,000. See D Birn, *The League of Nations Union 1918–45* (Oxford University Press: 1981) pp 24, 48.

4: Conciliation or Coercion? The Development of the League in the 1920s

1. S de Madariaga, *Disarmament* (Oxford University Press: 1929) p 20.

2. S de Madariaga, *Morning Without Noon* (Saxon House, DC Heath: 1973) p 33.

3. See Chapter 2, pp 35–6.

4. B Glazebrook, *Canada at the Peace Conference* (Oxford University Press: 1942) pp 67–71.

5. House of Commons, 21 July 1919.

6. DBFP Vol IX, p 76, minute by Curzon at the end of a memorandum by Sir James Headlam-Morley, Feb 1920.

7. L P Bloomfield, *Evolution or Revolution? The United Nations and the Problem of Peaceful Territorial Change* (Harvard University Press: 1957) pp 44–6.

8. Lord Robert Cecil, 'The League of Nations as a Historical Fact', in W Rappard, *Problems of Peace* (Allen & Unwin: 1935) See also Lord Robert Cecil, *The Moral Basis of the League of Nations* (Lindsey Press: 1923) p 28.

9. Memorandum by General Cockerill, undated, probably late 1918, FO 371/4366.

10. Walters, *A History of* the *League of Nations*, p 148.

11. British Cabinet meeting, 28 Oct 1925, Cab 23/51. See also J Barros, *The League of Nations and the Great Powers: The Greek-Bulgarian Incident of 1925* (Oxford University Press: 1970).

12. Cecil to Baldwin, 1 Sept 1923, Cecil Papers, 51080.

13. Curzon to Cecil, 1 Sept 1923, FO 371/9452; Curzon to Baldwin, 1 Sept 1923. Baldwin papers, quoted in K Middlemas and J Barnes, *Baldwin* (Weidenfeld and Nicolson: 1969) p 195.

14. For a detailed account of the crisis, see J Barros, *The Corfu Incident of 1923: Mussolini and the League of Nations* (Princeton University Press: 1965).

15. Admiralty to Foreign Office, 10 Aug 1927, FO 371/12674. Barros, *The Corfu Incident*, p 180.

16. 14 Sept 1923, Cecil papers 51126. Memo by Sir Eric Drummond, 14 Sept 1923, quoted in Barros, *The Corfu Incident*, pp 317–20.

17. Memo by Foreign Office official Villiers, July 1923, FO 371/11070.

18. *The Times*, 5 July 1922.

19. D Marquand, *Ramsay MacDonald* (Jonathan Cape: 1977) p 352.

20. 6th Plenary meeting of League Assembly, 4 Sept 1924, Assembly Records pp 41–6.

21. H Swanwick, *I Have Been Young* (Gollancz: 1935) p 401. See R Henig, 'The British Government and the League of Nations, 1919–26', unpublished Ph.D thesis, Lancaster University, September 1978, pp 296–300.

22. League Council, 12 March 1925, League *Official Journal* VI, p 445.
23. British Cabinet meeting, 20 March 1925, Cab 23/49.
24. S Marks, *The Illusion of Peace: International Relations in Europe 1918–33* (Macmillan: 1976) p 71.
25. Northedge, *The League of Nations: Its Life and Times*, p 97.
26. Marks, *The Illusion of Peace*, p 10.
27. Walters, *A History of the League of Nations*, p 385.
28. Walters, *A History of the League of Nations*, p 201.

5: The League and Disarmament

1. Lord Grey, *Twenty Five Years*, pp 91–2.
2. Extract from memorandum on German Obligations to Disarm, Lord Cecil, 5 March 1926, FO 371/11878.
3. S de Madariaga, *Disarmament*, pp 12–13.
4. Lord Cecil, *A Great Experiment* (Jonathan Cape: 1941) pp 78–9.
5. Eyre Crowe, Notes on Cecil's 'Proposals for the Maintenance of Future Peace', 12 Oct 1916, Cab 29/1.
6. A Webster, 'Making Disarmament Work', in C Fischer and A Sharp, *After the Versailles Treaty* (Routledge: 2008), p 136.
7. Webster, 'Making Disarmament Work', p 136.
8. Lord Esher to H A L Fisher, 21 Dec 1921, Lloyd George Papers F 16/7/76.
9. See J Wheeler-Bennett, *The Reduction of Armaments* (Allen & Unwin: 1925) p 58 for the full table.
10. R Brett and Oliver, Viscount Esher (ed), *The Journals and Letters of Reginald, Viscount Esher*, 4 vols (London: 1934–8) Vol IV, p 281.

11. The League of Nations, *Ten Years of World Co-operation* (Secretariat of the League of Nations: 1930) pp 56–7.

12. See Chapter 4.

13. Webster, 'Making Disarmament Work', pp 138–45.

14. Webster, 'Making Disarmament Work', p 145. See also Wheeler-Bennett, *The Reduction of Armaments*, pp 48–57.

15. Webster, 'Making Disarmament Work', pp 144, 146.

16. Lord Cecil, *A Great Experiment*, p 179; Webster, 'Making Disarmament Work', pp 140–2, 145.

17. D Richardson, *The Evolution of British Disarmament Policy in the 1920s* (1989) p 47.

18. Walters, *A History of the League of Nations*, pp 364–5.

19. C J Kitching, *Britain and the Problem of International Disarmament 1919–34* (Routledge: 1999) pp 96–7; Richardson, *Evolution of British Disarmament Policy*, p 88.

20. A Adamthwaite, *Grandeur and Misery: France's Bid for Power in Europe 1914–1940* (Arnold: 1995) pp 126–7.

21. Richardson, *Evolution of British Disarmament Policy*, p 60.

22. De Madariaga, *Morning Without Noon*, pp 87, 90.

23. Kitching, *Britain and the Problem of International Disarmament*, p 100.

24. For more detail on the Geneva naval conference of 1927, see Kitching, *Britain and the Problem of International Disarmament*, pp 97–109 and C Hall, *Britain, America and Arms Control 1921–37* (Macmillan: 1987) pp 43–54.

25. Walters, *A History of the League of Nations*, pp 371–2; Kitching, *Britain and the Problem of International Disarmament*, pp 111–12

26. Walters, *A History of the League of Nations*, p 439.
27. Z Steiner, *The Lights That Failed: European International History 1919–33* (Oxford University Press: 2005) p 776.
28. Steiner, *The Lights That Failed*, pp 786, 792.
29. MacDonald described it to King George V as a 'stop-gap designed not to achieve disarmament, but to prop up a conference which everyone knew to be disintegrating.' Quoted in C Kitching, 'The Search for Disarmament: Anglo-French Relations 1929–34' in A Sharp and G Stone (ed), *Anglo-French Relations in the 20th century* (Routledge: 2000) p 171.
30. S Steiner, *The Lights That Failed*, p 812.

6: The Manchurian Crisis, 1931–3

1. C Thorne, *The Limits of Foreign Policy – The West, The League and the Far Eastern Crisis of 1931–1933* (Macmillan: 1972) pp 44, 177.
2. Thorne, *The Limits of Foreign Policy*, p 61.
3. Thorne, *The Limits of Foreign Policy*, pp 142, 153.
4. R Storry, *The Double Patriots, A Study in Japanese Nationalism* (Cambridge: 1956) pp 101–2.
5. Documents on British Foreign Policy, (2nd Series), Vol VIII, 524, 647, 654.
6. Documents on British Foreign Policy, (2nd Series), Vol VIII, 621, 12 Oct 1931.
7. Thorne, *The Limits of Foreign Policy*, pp 170–1.
8. Documents on British Foreign Policy, (2nd Series), Vol VIII, 685.
9. Thorne, *The Limits of Foreign Policy*, pp 187–9.
10. Steiner, *The Lights That Failed*, pp 729–30.
11. Thorne, *The Limits of Foreign Policy*, pp 80–1.

12. Thorne, *The Limits of Foreign Policy*, p 162.
13. General C Dawes, *Journal as an Ambassador to Great Britain* (New York: 1939) pp 415–16.
14. Thorne, *The Limits of Foreign Policy*, p 76.
15. Thorne, *The Limits of Foreign Policy*, pp 123, 247.
16. Thorne, *The Limits of Foreign Policy*, p 209.
17. Thorne, *The Limits of Foreign Policy*, p 212.
18. Thorne, *The Limits of Foreign Policy*, p 204.
19. Thorne, *The Limits of Foreign Policy*, p 282.
20. Thorne, *The Limits of Foreign Policy*, p 283–4.
21. Thorne, *The Limits of Foreign Policy*, p 333.
22. Henig (ed), *The League of Nations*, p 106.
23. For more on this dispute see Walters, *A History of the League of Nations*, pp 525–36.

7: The Abyssinian Disaster

1. P Guillen, 'Franco-Italian Relations in Flux, 1980 – 40', in R Bryce (ed), *French Foreign and Defence Policy 1918–40* (Routledge: 1998) p 156.
2. Walters, *A History of the League of Nations*, p 397.
3. De Madariaga, *Morning Without Noon*, p 341.
4. Northedge, *The League of Nations: Its Life and Times*, p 226.
5. D Dutton, *Sir John Simon* (Arum: 1992) pp 204–5.
6. Northedge, *The League of Nations: Its Life and Times*, p 229.
7. Simon to Lord Cecil, June 1932, F.O. 800/287.
8. Northedge, *The League of Nations: Its Life and Times*, pp 229–30.
9. Northedge, *The League of Nations: Its Life and Times*, pp 230–1.
10. Cabinet meeting, 2 October 1935, Cab 23/82.

11. M Clark, *Modern Italy 1871–1982* (Longman: 1984) p 282.

12. Northedge, *The League of Nations: Its Life and Times*, p 233.

13. Northedge, *The League of Nations: Its Life and Times*, pp 238–9.

14. Northedge, *The League of Nations: Its Life and Times*, pp 241–2.

15. Dutton, *Sir John Simon*, p 232.

16. Dutton, *Sir John Simon*, pp 232–3.

17. Dutton, *Sir John Simon*, p 233; Northedge, *The League of Nations: Its Life and Times*, p 242.

18. In his book *Facing the Dictators*, Antony Eden wrote (of a meeting with King George V): 'He added: "I said to your predecessor: you know what they are all saying, no more coals to Newcastle, no more Hoares to Paris." The fellow didn't even laugh.' See The Earl of Avon, *The Eden Memoirs: Facing the Dictators* (Cassell: 1962), p 317.

19. Thorne, *The Limits of Foreign Policy*, p 388.

20. R A C Parker, *Chamberlain and Appeasement* (Macmillan: 1993) pp 60–1.

21. Northedge, *The League of Nations: Its Life and Times*, p 245.

22. Northedge, *The League of Nations: Its Life and Times*, p 245.

8: The League and the Development of International Society

1. D Laqua (ed), *Internationalism Reconfigured: Transnational Ideas and Movements between the World*

Wars (I.B. Tauris: 2011) pp 191–3, hereafter Lacqua, *Internationalism Reconfigured*.

2. For further information on the League of Nations Union in Great Britain, see D Birn, *The League of Nations Union 1918–1945* (Oxford University Press: 1981).

3. P Clavin, 'Conceptualising Internationalism', in Lacqua, *Internationalism Reconfigured*, p 7.

4. See J Barros, *Office Without Power* (Clarendon Press: 1979) and *Betrayal From Within: Joseph Avenol, Secretary-General of the League of Nations 1933–1940* (Yale University Press: 1969).

5. A Sharp, *The Versailles Settlement*, p 115.

6. A Sharp, *The Versailles Settlement*, p 33.

7. A Sharp, *The Versailles Settlement*, p 157.

8. Walters, *A History of the League of Nations*, p 175.

9. S L Hoffman (ed), *Human Rights in the Twentieth Century* (Cambridge University Press: 2011).

10. A Sharp, *The Versailles Settlement*, pp 159–165.

11. For a full account, see S Pedersen, *The Guardians: The League of Nations and the Crisis of Empire* (Oxford University Press: 2015), hereafter Pedersen, *The Guardian*.

12. J D Armstrong, L Lloyd and J Redmond, *From Versailles to Maastricht: International Organisation in the Twentieth Century* (St Martin's Press: 1996) pp 51–2, hereafter Armstrong, Lloyd and Redmond, *From Versailles to Maastricht*; Walters, *A History of the League of Nations*, pp 171–3.

13. Leonard Smith, *Sovereignty at the Paris Peace Conference of 1919* (Oxford University Press: 2018) pp 47–8.

14. Pedersen, *The Guardians*, p 405.

15. Walters, *A History of the League of Nations*, pp 187–9.
16. P Clavin, 'Europe and the League of Nations', in Robert Gerwath (ed), *Twisted Paths: Europe 1914–1945* (Oxford University Press: 2007) p 329, hereafter Gerwath, *Twisted Paths*.
17. D Gorman, *The Emergence of International Society in the 1920s* (Cambridge University Press: 2012) p 183. The Rockefeller Foundation supported the League's health work to the tune of $100,000 a year in the 1930s, and in 1933 contributed $135,000 to the Financial Section and the Economic Intelligence Service for a five-year study into the worldwide impact of the Depression on industrial production and banking laws. See Kuehl and Dunn, *American Internationalists and the League of Nations,* p 145.
18. Barbara Metzger, quoted in D Laqua, *Internationalism Reconfigured*, p 94.
19. D Laqua, *Internationalism Reconfigured*, pp 149–55.
20. D Laqua, *Internationalism Reconfigured*, p 149.
21. For an excellent general account of economic and financial relations between the United States, Britain and France in the inter-war period, see Robert Boyce, *The Great Interwar Crisis and the Collapse of Globalization* (Palgrave Macmillan: 2009).
22. P Clavin, *Securing the World Economy: The Reinvention of the League of Nations 1920–46* (Oxford University Press: 2013) p 35, hereafter Clavin, *Securing the World Economy*.
23. Clavin, *Securing the World Economy*, p 250–1.
24. P Clavin, 'Europe and the League of Nations', in Gerwath, *Twisted Paths*, pp 338–9.
25. Walters, *A History of the League of Nations*, pp 190–2.

26. Walters, *A History of the League of Nations*, p 170.
27. Armstrong, Lloyd and Redmond, *From Versailles to Maastricht*, pp 49–50.
28. Clavin, *Securing the World Economy*, p 10.

9: The League is Dead: Long Live the United Nations

1. Sir Alexander Cadogan, quoted in Armstrong, Lloyd and Redmond, *From Versailles to Maastricht*, p 62.
2. Alexander Loveday, Director of the Financial Section of the League, quoted in Clavin, *Securing the World Economy*, p 326.
3. Armstrong, Lloyd and Redmond, *From Versailles to Maastricht*, p 64.
4. Lord Cecil, 4 April, 1946, League of Nations *Official Journal*, 1946.
5. S Pedersen, 'Back to the League of Nations', in *American History Review*, Vol 112, No 4 (Oct 2007).

President Wilson's Fourteen Points, 8 January 1918

The program of the world's peace, therefore, is our program; and that program, the only possible program, as we see it, is this:

I. Open covenants of peace, openly arrived at, after which there shall be no private international understandings of any kind but diplomacy shall proceed always frankly and in the public view.

II. Absolute freedom of navigation upon the seas, outside territorial waters, alike in peace and in war, except as the seas may be closed in whole or in part by international action for the enforcement of international covenants.

III. The removal, so far as possible, of all economic barriers and the establishment of an equality of trade conditions among all the nations consenting to the peace and associating themselves for its maintenance.

IV. Adequate guarantees given and taken that national armaments will be reduced to the lowest point consistent with domestic safety.

V. A free, open-minded, and absolutely impartial adjustment of all colonial claims, based upon a strict observance of the principle that in determining all such questions of sovereignty the interests of the populations concerned must have equal weight with the equitable claims of the government whose title is to be determined.

VI. The evacuation of all Russian territory and such a settlement of all questions affecting Russia as will secure the best and freest cooperation of the other nations of the world in obtaining for her an unhampered and unembarrassed opportunity for the independent determination of her own political development and national policy and assure her of a sincere welcome into the society of free nations under institutions of her own choosing; and, more than a welcome, assistance also of every kind that she may need and may herself desire. The treatment accorded Russia by her sister nations in the months to come will be the acid test of their good will, of their comprehension of her needs as distinguished from their own interests, and of their intelligent and unselfish sympathy.

VII. Belgium, the whole world will agree, must be evacuated and restored, without any attempt to limit the sovereignty which she enjoys in common with all other free nations. No other single act will serve as this will serve to restore confidence among the nations in the laws which they have themselves set and determined for the government of their relations with one another. Without this healing act the whole structure and validity of international law is forever impaired.

VIII. All French territory should be freed and the invaded portions restored, and the wrong done to France by Prussia in 1871 in the matter of Alsace-Lorraine, which has unsettled the peace of the world for nearly fifty years, should be righted, in order that peace may once more be made secure in the interest of all.

IX. A readjustment of the frontiers of Italy should be effected along clearly recognizable lines of nationality.

X. The peoples of Austria-Hungary, whose place among the nations we wish to see safeguarded and assured, should be accorded the freest opportunity to autonomous development.

XI. Rumania, Serbia, and Montenegro should be evacuated; occupied territories restored; Serbia accorded free and secure access to the sea; and the relations of the several Balkan states to one another determined by friendly counsel along historically established lines of allegiance and nationality; and international guarantees of the political and economic independence and territorial integrity of the several Balkan states should be entered into.

XII. The Turkish portion of the present Ottoman Empire should be assured a secure sovereignty, but the other nationalities which are now under Turkish rule should be assured an undoubted security of life and an absolutely unmolested opportunity of autonomous development, and the Dardanelles should be permanently opened as a free passage to the ships and commerce of all nations under international guarantees.

XIII. An independent Polish state should be erected which should include the territories inhabited by indisputably Polish populations, which should be assured a free and secure access to the sea, and whose political and economic independence and territorial integrity should be guaranteed by international covenant.

XIV. A general association of nations must be formed under specific covenants for the purpose of affording mutual guarantees of political independence and territorial integrity to great and small states alike.

Founder Members of the League

Argentine
   Republic
Australia
Belgium
Bolivia
Brazil
United Kingdom
   of Great
     Britain and
     Northern
     Ireland
Canada
Chile
China
Colombia
Cuba

Czechoslovakia
Denmark
France
Greece
Guatemala
Haiti
Honduras
India
Italy
Japan
Liberia
Netherlands
New Zealand
Nicaragua
Norway
Panama

Paraguay
Persia
Peru
Poland
Portugal
Romania
Salvador
Siam
South Africa
Spain
Sweden
Switzerland
Uruguay
Venezuela
Yugoslavia

Further Reading

The most comprehensive chronological account of the League is still F P Walters' 800-page *A History of the League of Nations*. Although written over 65 years ago, the author's inside knowledge of the day-to-day workings of the organisation, as a member of the League Secretariat, makes this account an indispensable reference point for any serious student of the League. More recent and accessible accounts are: from Britain, F S Northedge, *The League of Nations: Its Life and Times*; and from the United States, Elmer Bendiner, *A Time for Angels: The Tragicomic History of the League of Nations*. A very comprehensive recent chapter on the League's activities by Patricia Clavin, 'Europe and the League of Nations', is contained in R Gerwarth, *Twisted Paths: Europe 1914–1945*, and an excellent reappraisal of the League's record as a peacekeeping body is contained in Susan Pedersen's review essay 'Back to the League of Nations' contained in *The American Historical Review* (October 2007). Zara Steiner's magisterial study of the 1920s and early 1930s, *The Lights that Failed: European International History 1919–1933*, covers the establishment and evolution of the League in considerable detail and with great insight, but unfortunately stops short of the Abyssinian crisis.

The impetus for the establishment of the League after the First World War is covered very comprehensively from the United States' perspective in Warren Kuehl, *Seeking World Order: The United States and International Organization to 1920*, and from the British perspective in George Egerton, *Great Britain and the Creation of the League of Nations*. A more recent addition on the British side is Peter Yearwood, *Guarantee of Peace: The League of Nations in British Policy 1914–1925*. The work of the League Commission in Paris is ably covered by Alan Sharp in *The Versailles Settlement: Peacemaking in Paris, 1919,* and by Margaret MacMillan in *Peacemakers: The Paris Conference of 1919 and its Attempt to End War*. A recent work focusing on the international legal aspects of the peace settlement is Leonard Smith, *Sovereignty at the Paris Peace Conference of 1919*. David Hunter Miller, the American delegation's legal adviser, published a verbatim account of the Commission's meetings in his two-volume *The Drafting of the Covenant* in 1928, and another member of the American delegation, Stephen Bonsal, captured the atmosphere and arguments at Paris relating to the League in his memoirs *Unfinished Business* and in his diary extracts contained in *Suitors and Suppliants*.

The chaos and instability of the post-war world in which the League started to operate is well captured by Robert Gerwath in *The Vanquished: Why the First World War Failed to End 1917–1923*. Two further excellent accounts of the ongoing problems of the 1920s and the divisions between the major powers are Robert Boyce, *The Great Interwar Crisis and the Collapse of Globalization* and Patrick Cohrs, *The Unfinished Peace after World War I*. In relation to the many specific crises faced by the League, three early incidents have been comprehensively analysed by James Barros in *The Aland*

Islands Question: Its Settlement by the League of Nations, The Corfu Incident of 1923: Mussolini and the League of Nations, and *The League of Nations and the Great Powers: The Greek-Bulgarian Incident, 1925*. The Manchurian crisis is definitively and exhaustively covered in Christopher Thorne, *The Limits of Foreign Policy: The West, the League and the Far Eastern Crisis of 1931–1933*. A succinct but very useful account of the Abyssinian disaster is contained in Frank Hardie, *The Abyssinian Crisis*, and the British public's response is well covered in Daniel Waley, *British Public Opinion and the Abyssinian War, 1935–6*. The League's decline after 1936 is analysed in an article by Peter Beck, 'The League of Nations and the Great Powers, 1936–1940', in *World Affairs* (Spring 1995) and is also covered in R A C Parker, *Chamberlain and Appeasement*.

There are a number of studies which focus on the League and disarmament. Andrew Webster's chapter, 'Making Disarmament Work: The Implementation of the International Disarmament Provisions in the League of Nations Covenant, 1919–1925' in *After the Versailles Treaty*, edited by Conan Fischer and Alan Sharp, is a very valuable summary of the League's early efforts in this area. Dick Richardson, *The Evolution of British Disarmament Policy in the 1920s*, focuses on the period 1924–9 and on the work of the League's Preparatory Commission for Disarmament, while Carolyn Kitching in *Britain and the Problem of International Disarmament: 1919–34* traces the League's attempts to link disarmament and security negotiations. There is also a useful article by Richardson and Kitching, 'Britain and the World Disarmament Conference', in *Britain and the Threat to Stability in Europe 1918 –45*, edited by Peter Catterall with C J Morris. Naval rivalry between the United States and Britain is ably covered by Christopher Hall in *Britain, America and Arms Control 1921–37* and by Captain Stephen Roskill in *Naval Policy Between the Wars, Volume I: The Period of Anglo-American Antagonism 1919–1929*.

There have been a number of recent books focusing on the League's technical, humanitarian, social and economic activities, and on the League's contribution to the emergence of a global society in the inter-war period. An excellent recent study of the League's supervision of mandates is Susan Pedersen's *The Guardians: The League of Nations and the Crisis of Empire*. A very full and detailed account of the League's financial and economic activities is contained in Patricia Clavin, *Securing the World Economy: The Reinvention of the League of Nations, 1920–46*. The ways in which the League laid the foundations for a global society are explored in three titles: Daniel Gorman, *The Emergence of International Society in the 1920s*; Daniel Laqua (editor), *Internationalism Reconfigured: Transnational Ideas and Movements between the World Wars*; and Akira Iriye, *Global Community: The Role of International Organizations in the Making of the Contemporary World*.

Popular opinion towards the League is covered in Donald Birn's *League of Nations Union, 1918–45* and in Martin Ceadel, *Pacifism in Britain, 1914–45: Defining of a Faith*. A good assessment of the League and of its contribution to the United Nations is contained in David Armstrong, Lorna Lloyd and John Redmond, *From Versailles to Maastricht: International Organisation in the Twentieth Century*. A recent study of the United Nations briefly covering the League of Nations is Paul Kennedy, *The Parliament of Man: The Past, Present and Future of the United Nations*.

Memoirs and biographies throw considerable light on the

evolution of the League and on the difficulties it faced, from the perspective of those who participated in its work and framed its policies. Lord Cecil's recollections are contained in two memoirs, *All the Way* and *A Great Experiment*, while Salvador de Madariaga's *Morning Without Noon* contains many interesting anecdotes. David Dutton's two biographies *Austen Chamberlain: Gentleman in Politics* and *Sir John Simon*, cover a number of important episodes in the League's history, and *The Austen Chamberlain Diary Letters,* edited by Robert Self, contains the correspondence of the British Foreign Secretary with his sisters Hilda and Ida in the 1920s. The policies of the Labour governments towards the League are covered in David Carlton, *Macdonald versus Henderson: The Foreign Policy of the Second Labour Government* and in David Marquand, *Ramsay MacDonald*. The League-related policies of the Lloyd George government are covered in Kenneth Morgan, *Consensus and Disunity: The Lloyd George Coalition Government, 1918–22*. Stephen Roskill's three-volume study *Hankey: Man of Secrets* has much useful information on British attitudes towards the League and on why Hankey turned down the offer of the post of League Secretary-General. James Barros has written biographies of both of the League's Secretary-Generals, *Office without Power* on Drummond, and in *Betrayal from Within* on Avenol.

Finally, the author would modestly like to mention a couple of her earlier books and articles which might be of interest: Ruth Henig (editor), *The League of Nations*, which is a collection of documents covering the history of the League; 'Britain, France and the League of Nations in the 1920s' in *Anglo-French Relations in the Twentieth Century: Rivalry and Cooperation* edited by Alan Sharp and Glyn Stone; and 'New Diplomacy and Old: A Reassessment of

British Conceptions of a League of Nations, 1918–20' in *The Paris Peace Conference, 1919: Peace Without Victory?* edited by Michael Dockrill and John Fisher.

Bibliography

Published Diaries, Letters and Memoirs

Amery, L S, *The Leo Amery Diaries: Vol I, 1896–1929, Vol II, 1929–1945*, ed J Barnes and D Nicholson (Hutchinson: 1980, 1988).

Bonsal, S, *Unfinished Business* (Michael Joseph: 1944).

———, *Suitors and Suppliants* (Prentice-Hall: 1946).

Cecil, Lord Robert, *A Great Experiment* (Jonathan Cape: 1941).

———, *All the Way* (Hodder and Stoughton: 1949).

Chamberlain, Sir Austen, *The Austen Chamberlain Diary Letters*, ed R C Self (Cambridge 1995).

Clemenceau, Georges, *Grandeur and Misery of Victory* (Harrap: 1930).

D'Abernon, Lord, *An Ambassador of Peace: Pages from the Diary of Viscount D'Abernon (Berlin 1920 – 1926)* (3 vols, Hodder and Stoughton: 1929–30).

De Madariaga, S, *Morning Without Noon* (Saxon House: 1973).

Grey, Lord, *Twenty Five Years 1892 –1916* (2 vols, Hodder and Stoughton: 1925).

Hankey, Sir Maurice *Diplomacy by Conference: Studies in Public Affairs 1920 – 1946* (Ernest Benn: 1946).

House, E, and C Seymour (eds), *What Really Happened at Paris* (Hodder and Stoughton: 1921).

Hunter-Miller, D, *The Drafting of the Covenant* (2 vols, G P Putnam's Sons: 1928).

Lansing, R, *The Peace Negotiations: A Personal Narrative* (Houghton Mifflin: 1921).

Lloyd George, D, *The Truth about the Peace Treaties* (2 vols, Gollancz: 1938).

Nicolson, H, *Peacemaking 1919* (Constable 1933).

Riddell, Lord, *Intimate Diary of the Peace Conference and After, 1918 – 1923* (Gollancz: 1933).

Salter, Sir J A, *Memoirs of a Public Servant* (Faber & Faber: 1961).

———, *Slave of the Lamp: A Public Servant's Notebook* (Weidenfeld & Nicolson: 1967).

Seymour, C (ed), *The Intimate Papers of Colonel House* (4 vols, Ernest Benn: 1928)

Stimson, H, *The Far Eastern Crisis* (Harper & Brothers: 1936).

Vansittart, R, *The Mist Procession* (Hutchinson: 1958).

Wilson, T (ed), *The Political Diaries of C. P. Scott 1911 – 1928* (Collins: 1970)

Secondary Sources

Adamthwaite, A, *Grandeur and Misery: France's Bid for Power in Europe 1914–1940* (Arnold: 1995).

———, *The Lost Peace: International Relations in Europe 1918–1939* (Arnold: 1980).

Alcock, A, *A History of the International Labour Organisation* (Macmillan: 1970).

Armstrong, J D, L Lloyd and J Redmond, *From Versailles to Maastricht: International Organisation in the Twentieth Century* (St Martin's Press: 1996).

Baer, G W, *Test Case: Italy, Ethiopia and the League of Nations* (Stanford University Press: 1976).

Baker, R S, *Woodrow Wilson and World Settlement* (3 vols, Doubleday, Page & Co: 1922).

Barker, A J, *The Civilising Mission: The Italo-Ethiopian War 1935–6* (Dial: 1968).

Barnett, C, *The Collapse of British Power* (Sutton: 1984).

Barnhart, M, *Japan and the World Since 1868* (Arnold: 1995).

Barros, J, *The Åland Islands Question: Its Settlement by the League of Nations* (Yale University Press: 1968).

———, *The Corfu Incident of 1923: Mussolini and the League of Nations* (Princeton University Press: 1965).

———, *The League of Nations and the Great Powers: The Greek-Bulgarian Incident, 1925* (Oxford University Press: 1970).

———, *Betrayal From Within: Joseph Avenol, Secretary-General of the League of Nations 1933–1940* (Yale University Press: 1969).

———, *Office Without Power* (Clarendon Press: 1979).

Beasley, W G, *Japanese Imperialism 1894–1945* (Oxford University Press: 1987).

Bendiner, E, *A Time for Angels: The Tragicomic History of the League of Nations* (Knopf: 1975).

Birn, D, *The League of Nations Union 1918–1945* (Clarendon Press: 1981).

Boemeke, M, G Feldman and E Glaser (eds), *The Treaty of Versailles: A Reassessment after Seventy-Five Years* (Cambridge University Press: 1998).

Boyce, R (ed), *French Foreign and Defence Policy 1918–1940: The Decline and Fall of a Great Power* (Routledge: 1998).

———, *The Great Inter War Crisis* (Palgrave Macmillan: 2009).

Butler, J R M, *Lord Lothian (Philip Kerr) 1882–1940* (Macmillan: 1960).

Carlton, D, *MacDonald versus Henderson: The Foreign Policy of the Second Labour Government* (Macmillan, 1970).

Catterall, P, with C J Morris, *Britain and the Threat to Security in Europe 1918–1945* (Leicester University Press: 1993).

Ceadel, M, *Pacifism in Britain 1914–1945* (Clarendon Press: 1980).

———, *Semi-Detached Idealists: The British Peace Movement and International Relations 1854–1945* (Oxford University Press: 2000).

Clark, M, *Modern Italy 1871–1982* (Longman: 1984).

Clavin, P, *Securing the World Economy: The Reinvention of the League of Nations 1920–46* (Oxford University Press: 2013).

Clayton, A, *The British Empire as a Superpower 1919–1939* (Macmillan: 1986).

Cohrs, P, *The Unfinished Peace After World War One* (Cambridge University Press: 2006).

Cowling, M, *The Impact of Hitler* (Cambridge University Press: 1975).

Cross, J A, *Sir Samuel Hoare: A Political Biography* (Cape: 1977).

Dockrill, M, and J Fisher, *The Paris Peace Conference: Peace Without Victory?* (Palgrave: 2001).

———, and D Goold, *Peace Without Promise: Britain and the Peace Conferences 1919– 1923* (Batsford Academic and Educational: 1981).

———, and B McKercher, *Diplomacy and World Power: Studies in British Foreign Policy 1890–1950* (Cambridge University Press: 1996).

Dobson, A P, *Anglo-American Relations in the Twentieth Century* (Routledge: 1995).

Dutton, D, *Austen Chamberlain: Gentleman in Politics* (Bolton: 1985).

———, *Sir John Simon* (Arum: 1992).

Egerton, G W, *Great Britain and the Creation of the League of Nations: Strategy, Politics and International Organisation 1914 – 1919* (Scolar Press: 1979).

Emmerson, J T, *The Rhineland Crisis, 7 March 1936* (LSE: 1977).

Fischer, C, and A Sharp, *After the Versailles Treaty: Enforcement, Compliance, Contested Identities* (Routledge: 2008).

George, A L, and J George, *Woodrow Wilson and Colonel House: A Personality Study* (Dover Publications: 1964).

Gerwath, R, *The Vanquished: Why the First World War Failed to End 1917–23* (Allen Lane: 2016).

——— (ed), *Twisted Paths: Europe 1914–45* (Oxford University Press: 2007).

Goldstein, E, *Winning the Peace: British Diplomatic Strategy, Peace Planning and the Paris Peace Conference 1916 – 1920* (Clarendon Press: 1991).

Gorman, D, *The Emergence of International Society in the 1920s* (Cambridge University Press: 2012).

Hall, C, *Britain, America and Arms Control 1921–1937* (Macmillan: 1987).

Hardie, F, *The Abyssinian Crisis* (Batsford: 1974).

Henig, R B (ed), *The League of Nations* (Oliver & Boyd: 1973).

Howard, H, *The Continental Commitment* (Penguin: 1972).

Iriye, A, *The Global Community* (University of California Press: 2002).

Jacobson, J, *Locarno Diplomacy: Germany and the West 1925–1929* (Princeton University Press: 1972).

Kennedy, P, *The Parliament of Man* (Allen Lane: 2006).

Kimmich, C, *Germany and the League of Nations* (Chicago University Press: 1976).

Kitching, C, *Britain and the Problem of International Disarmament* (Routledge: 1999).

Kuehl, W, *The United States and International Organisation to 1920* (Vanderbilt University Press: 1969).

———, and Dunn, *Keeping the Covenant: American Internationalists and the League of Nations 1920 –1939* (Kent State University Press: 1997).

Laqua, D (ed), *Internationalism Reconfigured: Transnational Ideas and Movements Between the World Wars* (I.B. Tauris: 2011).

Lentin, A, *Lloyd George and the Lost Peace: From Versailles to Hitler* (Palgrave: 2001).

Leventhal, F M, *Arthur Henderson* (Manchester University Press: 1989).

McKercher, B (ed), *Anglo-American Relations in the 1920s: The Struggle for Supremacy* (Macmillan: 1991).

MacMillan, M, *Peacemakers: The Paris Conference of 1919 and Its Attempt to End War* (Murray: 2001).

Marder, A J, *From the Dardanelles to Oran: Studies of the British Navy in War and Peace 1915–1940* (Oxford University Press: 1974).

Marks, S, *The Illusion of Peace: International Relations in Europe 1918–1933* (Macmillan: 1976).

Marquand, D, *Ramsay MacDonald* (Cape: 1977).

Mayer, A J, *The Politics and Diplomacy of Peacemaking* (Weidenfeld and Nicolson: 1968).

Middlemas, K, and J Barnes, *Baldwin* (Weidenfeld & Nicolson: 1969).

Morgan, K O, *Consensus and Disunity: The Lloyd George Coalition Government 1918–1922* (Clarendon Press: 1979).

Murray, G, *From League to United Nations* (Oxford University Press: 1948).

Noel-Baker, P, *The First World Disarmament Conference 1932–33 and Why it Failed* (Pergamon: 1979).

Northedge, F S, *The League of Nations: Its Life and Times 1920–1946* (Leicester University Press: 1986).

———, *The Troubled Giant: Britain Among the Great Powers 1916–1939* (G Bell & Sons: 1966).

Orde, A, *Great Britain and International Security 1920–1926* (Royal Historical Society: 1978).

Parker, R A C, *Chamberlain and Appeasement* (Macmillan: 1993).

Pedersen, S, *The Guardians: The League of Nations and the Crisis of Empire* (Oxford University Press: 2015).

Peters, A R, *Anthony Eden at the Foreign Office 1931–1938* (St Martin's Press: 1986).

Richardson, R, *The Evolution of British Disarmament Policy in the 1920s* (Pinter: 1989).

Rose, K, *The Later Cecils* (Weidenfeld and Nicolson: 1975).

Roskill, S, *British Naval Policy Between the Wars*: Volume I: *The Period of Anglo-American Antagonism 1919–29* (Collins: 1968).

———, *Hankey: Man of Secrets* (3 vols, Collins: 1970–4)

Scott, G, *The Rise and Fall of the League of Nations* (Hutchinson: 1973).

Sharp, A J, *The Versailles Settlement: Peacemaking in Paris, 1919* (Macmillan: 1991).

———, and G Stone (eds), *Anglo-French Relations in the Twentieth Century: Rivalry and Cooperation* (Routledge: 2000).

Sluga, G, *Internationalism in the Age of Nationalism* (University of Pennsylvania Press: 2013).

Smith, L, *Sovereignty at the Paris Peace Conference of 1919* (Oxford University Press: 2018).

Steiner, Z, *The Lights That Failed: European International History 1919–1933* (Oxford University Press: 2005).

Storry, R, *The Double Patriots: A Study in Japanese Nationalism* (Houghton Mifflin: 1957).

Temperley, H W V, *A History of the Peace Conference of Paris* (6 vols, Oxford University Press: 1920–4).

Thorne, C, *The Limits of Foreign Policy: the League, the West and the Far Eastern Crisis of 1931 –33* (Macmillan: 1972).

Waley, D, *British Public Opinion and the Abyssinian War 1935 – 1936* (LSE: 1975).

Walters, F P, A *History of the League of Nations* (Oxford University Press: 1952).

Wheeler-Bennett, Sir J, *The Disarmament Deadlock* (Routledge: 1934).

———, *Information on the Reduction of Armaments* (G Allen & Unwin: 1925).

———, *Disarmament and Security since Locarno 1925–1931* (Allen & Unwin: 1932).

Whittaker, D J, *The United Nations in the Contemporary World* (Routledge: 1997).

Yearwood, P, *Guarantee of Peace: The League of Nations in British Policy 1914–1925* (Oxford University Press: 2009).

Young, J W, *Britain and the World in the Twentieth Century* (Arnold: 1997).

Zimmern, A E, *The League of Nations and the Rule of Law* (Macmillan: 1936).

Index